Our Fathers.

The Phenomenon of Children

of Catholic Priests and Religious.

Vincent Doyle.

Published in 2020 by FeedARead.com Publishing

First Edition

A CIP catalogue record for this title is available from the British

Library.

To Emer.

For your patience, dedication and understanding,

'thank you', seems insufficient.

However,

from the bottom of my heart,

I am so grateful for you and all that you are.

You inspire me.

"From the very first moment of conception,

every child is eternally intended by God

to share in the Resurrection and become a citizen of the

kingdom of heaven.

This includes the children of the ordained."

(Father Oliver Treanor., 2020.)

Contents.

Prologue.   11

i.   **Chapter One.**

Understanding.   25

ii.   **Chapter Two.**

Out of Darkness.   83

iii.   **Chapter Three.**

The Moral Argument falls Apart.   123

iv.   **Chapter Four.**

Parēns.   166

v.   **Chapter Five.**

Viri Probati.   220

vi.   **Chapter Six.**

Using Coping International.   258

Epilogue   307

Key Terms   313

Bibliography.   315

Prologue.

I wish to take you on a journey. We will have to choose our footsteps carefully, you and me. We will step over, above and through the rock where Christ established His Church. We are in search of something, or rather someone, the priest's child. We cannot fall into those tired arguments that choirs of secularists cry - the abolition of celibacy, misunderstanding what celibacy is - a ban on marriage, not a ban on sexual activity, directly at least. The latter is chastity, through the two are juxtaposed.

However, we each have to take personal responsibility for what we do freely and knowingly. This includes the decisions we make about our relationships. The situation is different, of course, for those who are subject to force or fear or emotional pressure. Our relationships have implications for others, including our children. The harm that flows from inappropriate or dishonest relationships has the potential to touch multiple generations, and that should make us think carefully about what we are doing.

This book is not primarily concerned with the rights or wrongs of such relationships in themselves, but rather with the difficulties experienced by children born of such unions, which must always be a key consideration.

This journey is one that will lead us through a finely woven fabric, interwoven by the institution of the Catholic Church over centuries, a belief that children of priests and religious do not exist, a principle twisted by those whose job it is to promote belief - belief in God.

Yet many obscure from view, children created by God, fathered by priests. This is a contradiction within Catholicism.

This fabric has three separate and tangled strands, sociology, psychology and finally, theology.

The fact that you are reading this book, to begin with, suggests a level of interest in this subject, perhaps shock, suspicion also? Reflect on your own beliefs surrounding this phenomenon, the children of priests. What up to this point did you believe? Did you ever think about it? Was this issue a part of your world?

For the most part, non-acknowledgement may have characterised how you considered children of priests, with the occasional indiscretion sprawled across a tabloid only to be forgotten by the next headline.

However, a darker world exists, veiled by history, lies and deception. I lived in this world though I was born into it, thus knowing no difference. This is a world that is buoyed by conditions, and if the child of a priest does not obey these scrupulous conditions, they are ostracised, to begin with. Harm and emotional abuse permeate the duration of their lives; harm is normalised for these people.

When I found out who I was, like Truman, I wanted out.

I refused to live in a world where my existence was characterised by obedience to rigorous conditions of silence.

Thus, I broke the silence and went to Rome to amend this secretive process.

This story recounts how I journeyed from Ireland to the Vatican and throughout the Catholic Church, to gain recognition.

Though it is not an acknowledgement of me per se, but of us, the children of priests, for I knew there had to be more?

It is only in the collective that individuals blend in, lest you wrongly believe that you are the only one!

In this world, no windows of transparency exist. No breeze of truth or light of acknowledgement graces the crib that cradles the children of the ordained and religious.

The term, the children of the ordained, is the most accurate term one may use when referring to children fathered by clergy, since it is the most inclusive, as it includes bishops, archbishops, cardinals and popes who have fathered children throughout history up to and including the present day.

Henceforth, the phrase 'children of priests' assumes the understanding of the children of the ordained inclusively.

Both terms, children of priests and children of the ordained will be used interchangeably throughout this book with each term being understood in equal measure.

The term 'and religious' is added to equally acknowledge children of religious, male and female, i.e., nuns, brothers, monks and so forth. Consequently, children of the ordained and religious and/or children of priests and religious.

Hidden and buried, these children are called profane names by uncaring people and are sadly viewed as a means to an end of desired secrecy, deception and historical denial. They are threatened, assaulted and manipulated,

"We are going to bury this." These are the words cruelly said in my presence to a priest's child by a family member. However, burying "this", priestly paternity, meant burying any chance of living a life minus the paranoia that accompanies maintaining a secret as big as this. This specific child suffered greatly, unnecessarily.

This child was to be buried in a graveyard of secrecy, with centuries of clay pounded on top of their coffin of eternal silence. There they would lie interminably in the cold, hard, ardent clasp of non-acknowledgement, paranoid with fear. Afraid they upset the applecart; they may have somehow let somebody know that they might have betrayed the secret they knew so well, since being in the womb.

Thus, paranoia breeds and cultivates in the darkened world imposed upon them, as dark as the perverse inversion of natural rights, supposed to accompany a child's existence.

The institution of the Catholic Church has long promoted the adult-centered sacrifice worn well by many, the chaste and celibate life.

However, when he or she fails in that regard when a priest or religious has sex, it is referred to as the "lamentable defection" a term used by a Pope Saint Paul VI in 1967. (Pope Saint Paul VI., 1967.)

Sex in the clerical and religious context is considered by some as defecting, lamentable. Consequently, so too conceptions of children of the ordained/religious, wrongly so.

For some, the child conceived personifies this contradiction and all that is lamentable with said act.

These parents are responded to institutionally with suspension and expulsion from their jobs in ministry.

That which is lamentable remains within the realm of the unspoken, deliberately so. Gradually the unspoken becomes unreal and what is unreal, thus, does not warrant a response.

Put simply, it does not exist, so there could be no problem. It's quite a clever tactic, deliberate non-acknowledgement.

This process, though subtle, is quite deliberate non-acknowledgement of the children of priests and religious, note the word "deliberate."

> "Turning away from children fathered by priests is simply not an option. As you wisely write, [referencing my initial letter to him], 'theirs is a pain characterised by non-acknowledgement.' [...] The children of priests deserve advocates with an unswerving commitment to the rights of such children, who must be at the centre of all decisions local Churches make in responding to these cases."
>
> (Cardinal Blaise J. Cupich., 2019)

The sociological aspect of this issue is the bones of the problem, psychology and theology are the blood and flesh of a body of neglect that weighs upon a body of people, who always have and will always exist, the children of the ordained/religious.

The popularised belief of the non-existence of the children of the ordained feeds a sense of absence and confusion, experienced by the child of a priest.

The child feels pulled in two ways. Their natural rights, sense of identity seeks truth, transparency and to acknowledge their self, fully and without limitation. Simultaneously they grow increasingly confused by the weight of secrecy imposed upon them; vicious secrecy inebriates the domestic environment of the child at conception, consequently denying natural rights. Henceforth, silencing children of the ordained and religious will be referred to as *Silentium* for short.

> *Silentium* refers to the process of silencing a child of an ordained person/religious with regard to the child's identity as the child of an ordained person/religious

Reflecting on the definition of *Silentium* above, we call to mind, the term, the children of the ordained, as the most accurate term that one may use when referring to children fathered by clergy. This term is the most inclusive, as it includes bishops, archbishops, cardinals and popes who have fathered children. The irony that priest's respond with the word "*adsum*" meaning 'present', at the time of ordination, yet some priest-fathers cannot say that same word to their child, is palpable.

Silentium like a snake invades the mind and heart of the child, nurturing all that is dark, confusing, and irrational in them, distracting them from natural and organic processes, from what might be deemed a natural life.

You may know a priest's child who seems distracted or preoccupied, inattentive. *Silentium* preoccupies the child and adult-child to the point where they can no longer see the maladaptive effects it has upon their life, developmentally and in other ways.

Silentium is cleverly disguised as privacy and what is good for the child to keep prying eyes away. However, *Silentium*, masked as being something natural for the child, is not a blanket of warmth and protection, but a fog that engulfs the child, imprisoning them in a cell of clerical embarrassment and canonical scandal. (cann. 277 §2) Conditional parenting, a form of emotional abuse., nurtures *Silentium*.

Formed by societal expectations that manipulate their destiny, the children of the ordained are navigated by adult-centered whims and spend a lifetime enslaved by societal expectations of silence and obedience.

In all of this, on the horizon, theology shimmers much like a mirage, theology that promotes pro-life, respect of life from the womb until tomb, promotion of natural rights of children and the child's right to be known by his or her biological parents and furthermore, to know their biological parents.

A family first theology that emerged from a Holy Family, who themselves had to flee tyranny following the birth of a child.

This theology, however, seems aloft, apart, detached from their existence, nurturing only white picket fenced families or the starving, those caught in famine or war.

But the child of the ordained, lives outside the Catholic Church, watching families, guided by a gospel, parade into Church, to be preached at, prayed with and supported by their biological fathers, indeed saved! Those who do the preaching often haven't the goodwill to feed or support their own child. This is not Christocentric, this is egocentric, and it must stop. So, take my hand, as we delve into centuries of knitted beliefs, woven with a thread of feigned theology, wrapped around the eyes, ears and mouths of those closest to our holy priests and religious, their secret children, - children that many prefer to believe, do not exist at all. However, not only do we exist, but we always will. The Vatican has confirmed, "it is the first time" that time such a study regarding children of priests and religious has been completed. (Ardura., 2020) Let us hope that this effort is the first among many to come, so that we, the children of the ordained and religious may finally be free and never be trapped ever again inside the misgivings of adults, church and society. The Holy See notes regarding the children of the ordained in 2020, the following.

> "There is a specific [...] indication from the last two Popes around the world to all the Bishops, and they know [...], very well, how they have to act and the fact that the priest needs to be a real father for the child." (Andrea Tornielli. Vatican Director of the Dicastery for Communications., 2020.)

These are the words of Andrea Tornielli, an exemplary journalist and the Vatican editorial director of the Dicastery for Communications. These words were said in my presence alongside Mr Dan Tierney, a producer with the BBC in Rome in 2020. The question remains, however, how does one actualise that which the last two popes have asked us to, what they have indicated, needs to happen? Children of priests and religious live in close proximity to a celibate world. Celibacy as a tradition is diluted by inauthentic chaste celibacy. Thus, if the tradition of chaste celibacy is ever to elevate itself beyond the confines of lamentable defection, the only path is via *Viri Probati*. In this both child and tradition are sanctified.

Within the Catholic church, the vast doors of tradition are painted, interminably with concerns of humanity and will inevitably close on the latest craze or "trends of fashion and the latest novelty." (Cardinal Joseph Ratzinger., 2005) That is why Catholicism is so essential to the resolution for the children of the ordained regarding the trend of stigmatisation that they endure, unjustly. The problems that these children experience, from a catholic pro-life perspective, regardless of one's belief, can never be condoned.

One can never marginalise, stigmatise, ostracise or condemn a child owing to the nature of his or her conception whilst claiming a catholic heritage or motivation. *Therein*, lies the institutional paradox. Thus, let us begin.

Chapter One.

Understanding.

Some years ago, I posted a link to a blog concerning children of priests. A woman responded beneath the link, "wash your mouth out with soap." The rude remark surprised me. My naivety quietly queried, "but then, I'd taste soap, and my father would still be a Catholic priest?"

One cannot undo the past, but one can learn from it.

In an era when we tear down statues that are a monument to hatred, in a similar attempt to disguise and hide that which we disdain, we dress up a child of a priest with our misgivings and point fingers at him or her, destroying the reminder of that which we dislike.

In this instance, the child of a priest represents defection for the Catholic Church, defection from chastity and celibacy, as some priests/religious secretly marry in civil ceremonies. Pope Saint

Paul VI in 1967 spoke of men who are unfaithful to celibacy and chastity referring to said instances as the "lamentable defection." (Pope Saint Paul VI., 1967.) This type of language is harmful and hurtful to children of priests and religious since it associates their conception with defection and connotes something or someone that is "lamentable." However, unintended this may be, "outside of wedlock", "unfaithful", "scandal" (Cann. 277 § 2) all are words that remind society that this situation is abnormal. This implied abnormality characterises the child, unfairly so, and resultantly, (to avoid this) the child is hidden.

One woman confessed to her child later in life what encircled her head, were the following sentiments, that she scribbled on crumpled paper and with trembling hand, then passed to her adult child.

> "You're someone who is not wanted. You are from a different world than us, a different place. You do not fit. Everything was fine, but then you came along, you little tramp. We don't want you, and we don't want you [being] part of anything. You just don't fit."

Is it any wonder these children struggle? The child's experience in the womb would shape their wellbeing as they developed. They experienced what the mother experienced. Thus, even in the womb, clericalism impacts the child in the womb. The child later came to understand the trauma they underwent in the womb as preverbal.

Thus, somatic, they imbibed every word, thought and feeling that surrounded their existence.

On that torn piece of paper, words written, leaving the mothers mouth like thick, black treacle, a social toxin was injected into the child. This is the swaddling embrace in the womb for the children of the ordained. The mother sometimes becomes a funnel that infuses the child with rejection and hatred.

Children being fathered by allegedly celibate and chaste priests and religious (not forsaking female religious as mothers) has happened and will always happen, across history. Children of priests and religious are inevitable, that is the primordial characteristic of these children. Priests are fathers, spiritually speaking, it is indeed "ingrained" in their nature.

"The desire to be a father is ingrained in all men, even priests, who are called to give life, care, protection to their spiritual children entrusted to them" notes Pope Francis. (Pope Francis., 2013)

The primacy of spiritual fatherhood often overshadows the very real presence of biological fatherhood on behalf of chaste and celibate priests.

From a psychosocial perspective, the belief system that children of priests and/or religious do not exist is so secure that some consider it impossible for a priest to become a father, confused and stuttering when such an assertion is made as if grappling to understand such a declaration.

I first found out about my own paternity in 2011, on the evening of what would have been my father's 72nd birthday, it was a Thursday. I knew him only as JJ, he was my Godfather, and I loved him with a love only a son could have, for his father. Whilst I went along with the Godfather role as a child openly, I internally suspected there was more to our closeness than met the eye. His death in 1995 hit me hard, for it was the grief of a child for his father. But I had neither the words nor maturity to voice the depth of my loss, for, after all, he was only a Godfather, not my biological father, or so I believed. Leafing through a 40-year-old folder of poems that same Thursday evening in 2011, 'Aer Lingus Jet, Saint Bridgit' fell upon the floor, a poem written by the priest whose memory sat nestled in the back of my mind.

The old worn pages had an aroma of maturity, the fine dust of time slipped off the page with ease, as I picked it up from the tiled kitchen floor in county Longford. The fire crackled. The words were profound, though countrified, rustic and had a charm to them that I internally and instantly recognised.

Reading the poem slowly, I felt something internally crack, a recognition, an awareness, and I knew … "he was my father, wasn't he?" I voice my newfound knowledge. A tear escaped my mother's eye, and the sense of relief that overcame me was like a prisoner's first breath of fresh, free air. Truth!

The news of my father, for me, meant looking out into the world for someone else like me. Children of priests, now I had a title, it was a thing, and I wanted to meet others like me. I could not find any, however.

I retreated to the west of Ireland and spent almost the next decade on Ireland's west coast. There is a ruggedness to the West Coast of Ireland, a ruggedness I associated with truth, unapologetic, rustic, raw truth. I spent months and years writing poetry and foraging out a career in care but still, I looked for children of priests - it seemed I was the only one in the world.

Then one day, sitting in my box, gaudy yellow coloured office in Galway, I picked up the phone and called the Apostolic Nuncio in Dublin. I told him that I was the son of a priest and wanted to meet him. I felt acknowledgement by the church would help.

Archbishop Charles Brown, former Apostolic Nuncio to Ireland kindly invited me to his residence on the Navan Road in Dublin in 2013. The Apostolic Nuncio is the Pope's representative in a country.

A courteous man, originally from New York, we get on well to this day and remain in touch, though he has now departed Ireland. I wanted somehow to navigate a path of pastoral and psychological care, to carve out a place of welcome from the stern wooden façade of the Catholic Church, for me and others like me.

I recognised that my biological father in his kindness toward me, even though I didn't know the truth as I was too young, was evocative of an underlying consideration that could be given to all children of priests, wherever they were across the world.

We just needed to let them know somehow, and the Vatican seemed to be the right place to start that journey.

Everything that I did was based on instinct and gut feeling.

Archbishop Charles and I would meet many times over the coming years at his Dublin base. We discussed my situation and children of priests globally. It seemed, the more I delved into this proverbial rabbit hole, the more I realised that very little attention had been focused upon this issue, despite consistent media attention, deservingly concentrating on other areas of abuse in the Catholic Church.

Archbishop Brown pointed me toward another Archbishop, the Archbishop of Dublin, Archbishop Diarmuid Martin. By now, it was 2013, and I had been meeting intermittently with Church figures, asking questions, probing around where perhaps, I should not have been. Regardless, I saw no need to stop.

Archbishop Diarmuid Martin has always been a pioneer of supporting victims of clerical abuse, and he is a man I admire. Without him, Coping would have never gotten off the ground. I will always be indebted to him. Coping was nurtured in those early days in the soil of neglect that became apparent, the more the issue was discussed. In an April 2019 interview, discussing a meeting with then, Cardinal Bergoglio, subsequently His Holiness Pope Francis, Archbishop Diarmuid mentioned children of priests and their wellbeing.

> "I'll always remember our meeting in Quebec. [...] The subject came up about priests who had children. The pope and [Cardinal] Hummes were saying that the natural right of a child to know their father was more important than the positive law of the Church and I was one of those who supported that." (McGarry, 2019)

The Archbishop was not paying mere lip service. He supported what became known as Coping International, Children of Priests International. He supported it much more than financially. He gave initial legitimacy, a listening ear. In many ways, he provided what all children of priests need, pragmatism juxtaposed alongside compassion.

Sitting in Drumcondra in an equally impressive reception room as that of his neighbour Archbishop Brown, Archbishop Diarmuid and I went on to meet and discuss and carve out the issue of children of priests over the coming months and years. Archbishop Diarmuid reflects upon our early meetings.

> "He came to tell me his personal story, about the fact that his father was a priest and that he was interested in following up the question of children of priests" Archbishop Martin confirmed, regarding our initial meetings in Dublin, in a 2019 interview with ABC Australia in 2019. (Martin., The Hidden Children of the Catholic Church | Foreign Correspondent, 2019)

The question of children of priests was for me, something that evolved, something that would organically unfold, revealing layer upon layer of concealed issues; issues that are as historic as the Catholic Church itself.

I had a sense that it was the social non-acknowledgement of this issue that underpinned the stigma, that gave marginalisation of children of priest's life, enabling it to foster harm over and over toward the children of priests and religious.

Italian Sociologist, Franco Ferrarotti, referred to as 'the father of Italian sociology' comments on this issue. I met with Franco Ferrarotti in Rome. We discussed issues surrounding the children of the ordained at length over coffee in the beautiful Roman sunlight.

> "I am convinced that the children of priests suffer from second-degree precariousness. Not only of the precariousness of an economic order but of a deeper discrimination, a wound not easily healed, in my opinion, because of an indelible stigma: it is the children of sin, destined, for their existence and independently of their will, to demonstrate the finitude and the limits of even the most sublime vocation. The children of priests are in fact the living proof of human sinfulness and at the same time the testimony of a biblical promise that has not been kept."
>
> (Ferrarotti, 2020)

The words "independently of their will" for me got to the heart of the issue. Indeed, the global Church historically has never addressed this issue before me. This promotes non-acknowledgement that is 'independent of the will of the children of the ordained.' Thus, preordained disposition on how to treat children of the ordained became ingrained within the social fabric of our collective consciousness as Roman Catholics. This was particularly true within the Irish context.

> "In the past, we thought that to be Irish was to be Catholic and nationalist. That must have left Irish Protestants feeling side-lined, but we gave little thought to that."
> (O'Sullivan., 2011)

Fr. O'Sullivan's juxtaposition of nationalism and Catholicism can be applied outside the Irish context when considering the global stigma that children of priest's face, with an enthusiasm that is reminiscent of nationalism.

If one acted in a manner contrary to the national Catholic faith in the past, or present in certain cultures, the response was and remained to be, social exclusion underpinned by the same passion that fuel nationalism.

To expel a child and call such an act ethical or holy is genuinely an offence against God.

This is true internationally today, in the context of the children of priests and religious. Such exclusion is believed to be for the good of the church and society, wrongly so. The social exclusion and marginalisation of the children of priests and religious, based on so-called Catholic values, evokes fanaticism within Catholicism. Criticism of the children of children of the ordained was and is masked as Catholic teaching, which of course it is not. In this, both Catholicism and the child are undermined.

The result, of the faith-based undermining of the children of the ordained and religious, with the same ardent desire that buoys nationalism, is guilt and shame. Fr. O'Sullivan notes in *Children, Learn What They Live*, citing a reflection by an unknown author.

> "Children who live with criticism learn to condemn. Children who live with hostility learn to fight. Children who live with ridicule learn to be shy. Children who live with shame learn to be guilty. [Fr. O'Sullivan concludes], the image of God that children come to have is substantially modelled on the image they have of their parents." (O'Sullivan, 2001.)

Therefore, it is wrong to forcefully place a negative image of childhood, creation, and life in the mind of a child, simply because it does not suit a particular agenda and to promote this as Catholicism.

To stigmatise a child is gravely harmful. Furthermore, to call such an act Catholic is to mislead and deceive. In doing so, you harm children "independently of their will" (Ferrarotti, 2020) Catholicism itself and the place you call home.

This stigma that has permeated Catholicism is as historic as it is harmful. Coping addressed the Pontifical Committee for Historical Sciences in 2020, headed by *Father Bernard Ardura*.

> **Doyle:** "Coping International is an organization dedicated to the care and mental health of the children of priests and religious. Prior to the work of Coping International, in your capacity as head of the Pontifical Committee for Historical Sciences, are you aware of *any* study on the issue of children of ordained priests and religious that is openly accessible to the public?"
>
> **Father Ardura:** "No, I had not been aware of any openly public study on this question."

Doyle: "In your opinion, is this the first time such a study has been done, Reverend Father?"

Father Ardura: "As far as I know, it is the first time."

(Ardura., 2020)

Thus, this is the "first time" according to the Vatican, "such a study has been done." What does this mean?

It means this issue lay dormant for centuries, deliberately so, thus enabling harm of thousands upon thousands of children of the ordained and religious.

For centuries, until now, clergy and religious (male and female) have been unfaithful to vows and promises made at ordination and consecration, begetting children, and latterly neglecting them in favour of the preservation of appearances. The conception of the children of the ordained and religious will inevitably continue in the future, as nature can never be wholly curbed by a tradition of sacrificing this part of human nature.

Yet amazingly the question of clerical paternity was never raised publicly?

The ecclesial sheen of the "brilliant jewel" of celibacy, a term used by Pope Saint Paul VI in 1967 in his encyclical *Sacerdotalis*

Caelibatus, indeed was and remained to be, "guarded by the Church for centuries" to the present day. (Pope Saint Paul VI., 1967.)

Thus, openly asking such questions, was going to be met with distancing, aggravation, and hostility since it was the first time the Catholic Church has publicly acknowledged the fruit of clerical indiscretion on such a mass level.

However, my meetings in Ireland with Church authorities and latterly, communications with the Irish Bishops Conference were always seasoned with honesty and openness, infused with a recognition of the inevitability of this issue as pressing and requiring attention. I wanted and still want this openness to be more global.

Archbishop Diarmuid Martin and Brown both recognised the importance of this issue. Archbishop Martin provided seed funding for the website www.copinginternational.com

The letters in the word Coping stand for children of priests international. The Archbishop had one request only, "we do this right."

Thus, a social unfolding of what was possibly one of the most closely guarded secrets in Church history began to see the light of day.

From my humble apartment in Galway's West end, as buskers lulled evenings in Salthill to a close, I sat with my laptop writing to the Bishops Conference and religious bodies in Ireland. Between 2003 and 2007, I had completed a Pontifical Degree of Theology at Maynooth College. This enabled me to speak with a theological proficiency in addressing the Bishops.

Why did I write to the Bishops of Ireland, were they and other church hierarchy globally, not the cause of the problem?

I have never been a big believer in picketing with signs and loudspeakers at gates of Churches, it rains in Ireland, and I was likely to get wet and ignored.

Moreover, a soggy, ignored child of a priest standing like a lonely puppy at the gates of some Bishop's house does not scream social justice to me.

Theologically speaking, from a pro-life perspective, the Catholic Church promotes respect for life at all stages, from the womb to the tomb. Thus, stigmatising or licencing and enabling a system of silence surrounding the existence of children of Latin rite priests and religious which cultivates psychological harm, is not evocative of a pro-life stance and this cannot be denied.

It is, however, a fact that is often sidestepped and distracted from by other issues.

I recognised that an internal crack, a contradiction stood glaringly in front of the whole world, the certainty of clerical paternity. However, this certainty was and continues to be responded to in a neglectful manner. Priests and religious, whose job it is to respect life, deny and silence their offspring, hence a contradiction in part. This was not only profoundly disingenuous to the natural rights of the child conceived in secret but also evocative of systemic hypocrisy when one claims to promote a pro-life ethos from a Catholic perspective.

By the end of 2013, I found myself back on the Navan road again, with Archbishop Brown. Plans were afoot with Archbishop Martin to create a website, a specifically devoted place for the children of priests to come, learn and recognise they were not alone.

"The Vatican Embassy is at your disposal, what can we do for you", Archbishop Brown said to me.

Archbishop Charles wanted to let me know that he was there to help in whatever way that he could. "I want to meet the Pope", I replied.

I glanced up as I awaited his response and saw a picture of Pope Emeritus Benedict XVI smiling tenderly at me, while the portrait of Saint John Paul II gazed down intently upon me from the high walls. The coffee the kind Religious Sister provided, as was customary, curled into the brief silence that fell between us. By this stage, Pope Francis was not even one year in office. "Why do you want to meet the Pope?" the Archbishop queried. "Because I want to get a blessing", I informed him, and I did. I wanted a blessing, a blessing upon the son of a priest who openly acknowledges his identity and who wanted to open this issue related to children of the ordained/religious.

The Archbishop kindly put in the request to Rome and some months passed. Then, one unusually bright afternoon in February 2014, a phone call came to my Galway home, it was the Archbishop from the Nunciature in Dublin. It was confirmed, I would be given a few moments with His Holiness the following June 2014.

The date was set, Wednesday, June 4th, which was the 19th anniversary of my father's death. "We thought it was appropriate", I was informed by the Archbishop. Months passed and then as if overnight, I was there, in Rome.

Historic Rome glowed all around me, welcoming me, glistening with antique reflections of centuries of history. Finally, Coping could seek a solution from the men who wandered the halls of the Vatican adorned with history and grandeur, some of whom created these long-forgotten children. This was 2014, the Vatican abuse summit on sex abuse would not happen for another five years, still under the Papacy of His Holiness Pope Francis.

The night before I met His Holiness, I sat by a window in my hotel room near the Vatican, starting at the dome of Saint Peter's that heaved beneath a navy-blue sky. The crown St. Peter's Basilica reached into an ocean of stars.

Tiny night lights glittered over Saint Peter's, as the magnificent dome heaved like a maternal breast in silence.

I was conscious of the Mariological theme enveloped within the structure that sat before me. I wondered, beneath this dome, is there a place for the hidden children, so psychologically hurt that they had to be banished to the dark shadowy depths of society and history? Would the Dome of Saint Peter's shelter in her heart, room for the most marginalised, their children, the children of her brother priests and sisters?

Is it possible for Catholicism be raised to such a mighty height to surrender to itself to the dignity of all children of the ordained/religious?

Can such people tend to the wounds inflicted upon tiny, socially invisible children?

To do so, would mean to crucify pride, clericalism and all adult-centered misgivings and tend to the lambs. It would mean being catholic, and as the Lord said, "by their fruit, you will know them." (Matthew 7:16.)

Pope Francis had the power to do nothing or ensure that something was done.

I did not sleep well that night, June 3rd, 2014, nor was I tired when I arose early to get ready to meet a Pope.

It was nineteen years to the day when I had stared into a grave dug by neighbours, lined with wildflowers, the final resting place of my deceased father.

Now I was staring at beautifully arranged flowers at the Vatican, whose purpose was different, not to mourn but to gratify and decorate.

My interpreter, Jhon Valencia from Colombia, accompanied me to meet with His Holiness.

Mr Valencia would speak to His Holiness in fluent Spanish.

He would interpret and explain the programme I had designed, Coping International, a platform for children of priests that facilitates free mental health globally, advocating for the rights of children of priests and religious, over the years pastorally and in other ways, supported by the Nuncio and church authorities in Ireland.

When we arrived at the Vatican, we were escorted to our seats, front row, approximately seventy-five feet from the place of the Pope. The sun rose, and His Holiness arrived into the crowds of people, who had gathered and assembled to catch a glimpse of Christ's Vicar on earth.

I stared at the giaont screens, grateful to God for this impending moment when it would just be, he and I, the son of a Catholic Priest, researching the psychological pains of thousands of other children of priests, and a sitting Pope.

When His Holiness arrived in Saint Peter's square, the crowd's collective voice bellowed in a powerful chorus of jubilation, rising with the sun into the bright Italian morning. It was almost like the Beatles at Shea Stadium, Saint Peter's Square simply erupted. The Wednesday audience was engaging, and I listened attentively. Still, my heart and mind were focused on the brief interlude that I would have with the most powerful human in the Catholic Church, Saint Peter's successor, after the Papal audience.

After the Bishops and Cardinal's had met the Pope, His Holiness approached where I stood attentively with Mr Valencia. His Holiness approached me after a few moments and reached out his hand to greet me. I embraced his extended hand and gently turned it over and kissed the Ring of the Fisherman.

His Holiness humbly stood as I held this moment, deep within my heart. I noticed the ring he was wearing was smaller than other Papal rinogs I had seen. It was silver and not gold and in no way adorned. I placed my left hand on his shoulder as by now. He was less than a foot from my face. His Holiness stood staring at me, awaiting a gesture or a word from me.

"*Soy el hijo de un sacerdote Irlandés*" I whispered. In Spanish, this means, "I'm the son of an Irish priest."

His Holiness' face turned toward me, (and he extended his ear,) he looked mildly perplexed. I believe I may have mispronounced some of the Spanish words, as I am not fluent in Spanish. I repeated. He paused and then smiled, nodding, indicating that he understood. I without delay introduced Jhon Valencia, my interpreter.

Pope Francis and I, Vatican City. June 4th, 2014.

His Holiness' body language did the rest. He turned to me and placed his arm around me. Mr Valencia began to speak to His Holiness about Coping International in fluent Spanish.

He informed His Holiness what Coping International meant, what Coping stood for and what the mission objectives of this organisation are.

Ultimately Mr Valencia, on my behalf, told His Holiness that Coping wanted to work with the Catholic Church not outside or against it. All that Catholicism stands for is what Coping stands for; that is, the intrinsic dignity of a child above all other considerations.

However, it remained, could the Catholic Church do this? Would human pride overshadow what the truly Catholic thing to do was? Mr Valencia further explained that Coping needed the help of the Vatican and the Papacy to achieve this. Mr Valencia handed a letter that I had written, translated into Spanish, to His Holiness. Attached to the message was a second letter, from the United Nations Children's Rights Commission which was addressed to the Archbishop of Dublin in his capacity as Vice-President of the Irish Bishops.

The second letter was a United Nations letter which referenced children of priests and the use of confidentiality agreements. This letter referenced a 2014 document released by the UN calling for better treatment of children of priests. The Pope held the two documents, reading the first page attentively, scanning it with a seriousness written all over his face. The letter I wrote referenced a phrase used by His Holiness, in his capacity as Cardinal Bergoglio written in 2010, in his book *On Heaven and Earth.*

> "If a priest comes to me and tells me that he has gotten a woman pregnant ... I remind him that the natural law comes before his right as a priest ... just as that child has a right to his mother, he has the right to the face of his father..." (Cardinal Jorge Bergoglio. , 2010)

The Pope looked over the letter for a moment, intently and turned to me, placing the message on his heart, smiling, he quietly said, "... *sí, sí,* I will read."

These are the only words uttered by His Holiness to us in our presence, but it was enough.

As a Psychotherapist, I was conscious of His Holiness' body language.

He remained entirely open to us, welcoming us, listening, remaining attentive, acknowledging, in no way aggressive, revolted or wishing to get away from us.

He gave us a parting gift, two rosary beads.

He would read our documents, this much I knew.

Holding them to his heart, His Holiness blessed us and began to leave. I gave a gift to the Pope, as is custom. Jhon and I turned into that June morning heat. "Coffee?" we unanimously asserted.

We would spend an hour in a café near the Vatican opposite the Sistine chapel breathing in what had just happened, considering what might happen next, if anything?

That date was June 4th, 2014.

The Irish Bishops would meet the following Monday, 9th June 2014, at the Conference of Catholic Bishops in Maynooth, Ireland.

Coping was on their agenda, the first Episcopal Conference in living history to openly acknowledge this issue of children of priests, to my knowledge, latterly publishing their deliberations.

I had informed the Pope that the Bishops of Ireland would meet the following Monday.

I wanted him to encourage his Irish Bishops. I wanted the Vatican and episcopal backing on this issue since the problem that I was trying to overcome was mammoth.

True to form, the Irish Bishops supported my plea for support, and they deserve enormous credit for this.

I wanted them to engage with Coping. Ultimately, I would elicit theology on the topic so the Catholic Church could officially do the right thing; no longer would the default of saying nothing and bury this mentality rule with superiority if the truth of Catholicism and pro-life shined brightly in the media. I wanted to theologically revert the default norm of ignoring as the right response to making non-acknowledgement of this issue to be considered anti-Catholic.

I would go on to write to the Bishops of Ireland for over six years, writing letters laden with theology, psychology, and sociology.

I did my absolute best to unpack what remained hidden from the everyday person walking beneath the window of my small apartment.

In 2015, I queried the ethical nature or lack thereof surrounding confidentiality agreements, legal strangleholds that silence children of priests.

Whilst the answer is glaringly obvious to any rational person, it was, and remains to be, vital to have an on the record ecclesial account of what is obvious. What is evident in no way negated neglectful behaviours and practices that invade the natural rights of children of priests until that point in history. Thus, the need for theological consensus.

In 2015, in what was possibly the first on the record condemnation of confidentiality agreements, imposed upon children of priests, the Bishops of Ireland, in this regard acknowledged, to their credit as follows.

"Such an agreement is unjust if, firstly, it compromises the consent of the parties involved. For example, if undue pressure is brought to bear on the mother. Secondly, such agreements may also be unjust if they hinder the basic goods of mother and child. For, example, if they are used primarily to protect the reputation of the priest or the institutional Church by creating a veil of secrecy that isolates the mother and child from relationships, knowledge and resources, which they are owed in natural justice." (Irish Catholic Bishops Conference., 2015.)

Now, anyone in the world could hold this letter in their hand before any bishop/superior, globally. What is a concern for a Catholic in Ireland, is of equal concern for other Catholics in other parts of the world!

I set about building a theological and pastoral mould that could be held up against the whole ecclesial world, alongside the simple question, "if the Irish hold this to be true, your brother bishops, why don't you?"

Now, we had episcopal backing, a website funded by the Catholic Church, a papal blessing that arrived in December 2014 assuring me of His Holiness' "appreciation for the [...] sentiments that motivate [Coping's initiatives.]" (Vatican Secretariat of State., 2014) This was a great start, but quantifiable evidence was missing.

By late 2014, early 2015, I was over halfway through completing a qualification as a psychotherapist.

At the beginning of my qualification, I was one day sitting with a colleague. I remember saying,

> "I can't be the only one" referring to me being the child of a priest, "there have to be thousands, right"?

This was one of many sparks that propelled me to the Irish Nuncio and Irish hierarchy in search of clarity, truth, and justice on this issue.

After I met with the Pope 2014, the website was launched in December 2014, just as the Pope's blessing was confirmed.

The website www.copinginternational.com launched without any international media coverage. The site funded entirely by Archbishop Diarmuid Martin would sit online, receiving no media coverage for almost three years. The reason was simple. I wanted to see how many people on a global level would seek out via online search engines, information related to this topic.

Thus, I wanted to compile qualitative and quantitative data concerning this phenomenon since no known data existed on the issue. The site, in a non-identifiable way, tracks unique visitors, countries where people access the site, and importantly and interestingly, key search phrases typed quietly into search engines online that brought people to Coping.

Below is a table of information (reprinted verbatim) amassed between Coping's launch in December 2014 and August 2017 when Coping's first international story, written by globally renowned journalist Michael Rezendes, for the Boston Globe. Rezendes' piece propelled the children of priests and religious into media headlines everywhere, immediately destroying the historic and default non-acknowledgement that surrounded our existence for centuries. The moment the Boston Globe hit American pavements; the ecclesial non-acknowledgement of this issue died.

Year	Unique Visitors.	Unique Key phrases used on search engines.
Dec. 2014	176.	N/A.
2015	3242.	• Children of priests. • Children born by Catholic priest. • Catholic priest's children. • Biological child of a priest. • My dad is a priest. • Catholic priests who are biological parents to children. • I am pregnant and the dad is a Catholic Priest.

2016	5397.	• Children of priests' rights. • Children fathered by priests. • Secret children of priests. • Catholic payment for children of priests. • Help, I am pregnant, and the father is a Catholic priest. • I am pregnant, and the father is a Catholic Priest
2017. Prior to 15/8/17	5051	• Catholic priests with children. • Human rights for children of priests. • Priests who have fathered children. • Catholic priests who father children. • Children fathered by Catholic priest. • Priests with kids. • My father is a Catholic Priest.

The key search phrases showed and confirmed that there were women (or girls in the case of sexual abuse of a minor) who were pregnant between the years 2014 – 2017. It confirmed that children of priests existed who were seeking out information on this topic. The figures confirmed that by August 2017, more than 13,000 people had come forward out of an incredible 175 countries seeking information on the subject of children of priests.

I refer to this period as 'the research period' of Coping's development.

Consider, if only 1 of every ten people who visited Coping's website between December 2014 and August 2017, before Rezendes' piece, is the child of a priest, that is still more than 1300 children seeking help. How many children do not have access to the internet? How many do not speak English? How many more are bullied into silence? How many have died?

Thus, it is apparent from Coping's statistics that thousands of priests and religious have fathered children, much more than 1300 children, considerably more.

To date, more than 150,000+ unique visitors have logged onto Coping and counting.

Again, if priests fathered only 1 in every ten who have logged onto the site, this equates more than 15,000 children of priests seeking help, information, and affirmation globally, and rising.

As Coping gets older, more people come forward, even if only .5% of the unique visitors to Coping are the child of a priest, as it stands, that's over 7,500 children of priests, many of whom believe, "I'm the only one."

Fr. Victor Kotze, with whom I have had the pleasure of conversing with via email, confirms in his 1987 Master's Thesis in Clinical Psychology degree that approximately 48% of clergy in South Africa at the time of writing in 1987 had casual sexual encounters.

> "48% (roughly) and, at the time of writing, had casual sexual encounters" (Kotze., 1987.)

Fr. Kotze commented further in response to my query, "did your statistics surprise you?"

> "The stats did not surprise me – it was there for all who opened their eyes and could see what the situation was/is. I also think that the study and other studies raise the important question of priestly celibacy and this is for the future of the Catholic Church – it is hard to think that those in authority – the Vatican and others – who in spite of these studies still object to married priests and those whom we call *Viri Probati* – and then there are hundreds who left to marry – and who would love to return to ministry. I pray it is the future of the Church." (Kotze, 2020)

Kotze's recognition of those "who would love to return to ministry" may see a light of hope concerning this aim, later on in this book.

As part of my research for this book, I did come across a statistic that cites "one in five" priests in the Philippines, having fathered children. In my experience, I believe the true figure could stand outside the "one in five" claim. Fr Jaime Achacoso, Professor of Canon Law and General Ethics, confirms, this statistic "cannot be substantiated." However, I was eager to gain clarification on possible numbers, regarding the children of the ordained in the Philippines, undoubtedly, an ongoing issue. Fr. Jaime Achacoso confides.

> "Once in a conversation with a Local Ordinary, [the Bishop] admitted to me that in his diocese he knew some priests involved with women, but he could not really discipline the errant priests, with the threat of them denouncing others who were in a similar situation. Pressed, he admitted that many other priests are in the same situation." (Fr Jim Achacoso, 2020)

Fr. Achacoso's statement points toward a systemic issue present in the Philippines, one the Catholic Bishops' Conference of the Philippines is eager to address compassionately.

David Rice, in his book *Shattered Vows*, published in 1992, confirms that almost 80% of priests in Peru have families. (Rice., Shattered Vows., 1992.)

> "I was given the reason that a man without a wife or family was not respected was despised as a *mula*--a mule. Therefore, priests had to marry to have any standing or authority in the community. I was also told that the Vatican knows this perfectly well, but turns a blind eye, as the alternative is no priests at all." (Rice., 2020)

Though this "blind eye" approach has begun to wane, viewing the issue truthfully on behalf of the entire church has yet to happen.

I find the representation of the priest without a wife, depicted as a *mula*, gravely disrespectful.

Nonetheless, it is only in understanding such cultural belief systems that we can peel back the reality that exists beneath purported and assumed clerical and religious obedience toward chastity and celibacy.

Rice further adds, "Germany's Catholic News Agency (KNA) on 30 January 1985, released the findings of a questionnaire administered to the clergy in the Archdiocese of Cologne and answered by 27 per cent of priests. No 13 of the questionnaire asked if these men believed 'a certain number of priests live celibacy only outwardly, and that, hidden from public view, they evade celibacy through numerous compromises [...]' Seventy-four per cent of the diocesan priests and 88 per cent of the order priests answered yes." (Rice., Shattered Vows., 1992.)

This is not an exhaustive list, South Africa, the Philippines, Peru, Germany, all these points toward one thing, the need for realism to be faced. This will help both the secret child and the celibate life if it is to continue and to do so healthily. As Sr. Maura O'Donohue once confirmed, in the context of abused female religious, "only if we can look at it honestly will we be able to find solutions." (John L. Allen Jr., 2001)

Peru, the Philippines, South Africa, and Germany, underpinned by the figures that Coping presents, point toward a hidden reality, global priestly and religious paternity veiled from public sight.

The oldest child Coping has met at the time was 94 years old. Her father was born more than 120 years ago, thus the focus quantitatively that spans more than a century. The youngest child, still in the womb. With 1600 religious leaving religious life in 2019 alone, how many live, in secret, promoting silence rather than wellness?

The information gathered by Coping was enough to convince the Catholic Church that this issue warranted attention. It was also enough to convince Michael Rezendes to do a story on it.

Now we had factual evidence to support what was suspected all along, now figures, statistics and visible data were presented to the world, now it could be proven beyond a reasonable doubt that priests have and continue to father children.

Giving this issue visibility via Coping's data was primarily about one thing, negating the imposed non-acknowledgement surrounding this phenomenon.

Dialogue with the Irish Bishops during Coping's research period (2014-2017) was about one thing, creating a viable response to the problem that was simultaneously emerging. Speaking to the Pope was about one thing, making this a concern for Catholics globally.

When the American media promoted the Irish pastoral mould to the world, for which I am so grateful, episcopal conferences everywhere saw a group of Bishops supported by the Pope, supporting the most marginalised children, the children of priests.

Irish episcopal backing, papal backing, confirmed global data all hit Boston pavements Wednesday, August 17th, 2017.

The Boston Globe front page read,

"a priest's son takes his case directly to the Pope."

This is the headline that graced the Globe that Wednesday morning. (Rezendes., 2017)

Rezendes appeared on 'CBS This Morning' in the United States to speak about the article, about Coping and Jim Graham, a man who would go onto exhume a Catholic priest from his grave to prove paternity. This effort proved to be fruitful and historic in equal measures.

Latterly it emerged that people are also using genealogy alongside home DNA tests to uncover clerical paternity. Linda Kelly-Lawless from Mount Gambier, Australia, used genealogy to discover the identity of her biological father.

More and more children of the ordained are digging up the past literally and via genealogy to find secrets once thought buried. Kelly-Lawless might be considered a pioneer in this regard, alongside Graham.

This was the beginning of what I viewed as turning the tide of silence, that had psychologically cascaded over the mouths and cradles of children of priests and religious for centuries. This was the beginning of a social movement that would allow children of priests to raise their head above water and recognise that they are not alone.

Emails and calls began and continue to come into the Coping office daily. The Church scrambled to respond, but the Irish Bishops would prove to be world leaders in terms of safeguarding the children of priests and religious. Ireland became the benchmark that other episcopal conferences and religious bodies sought to mimic. Even the Vatican has praised them, in my presence.

Tales of priestly and religious indiscretions flooded our inbox; priests with multiple children, priests who secretly married in different countries, whilst maintaining an outwardly celibate, unmarried identity in another.

Nuns and priests, cardinals and archbishops, nobody is exempt. This is what makes this scandal that graced the Church unique in that, with other scandals, one can rightly condemn the act (when a crime has been committed, etc.). However, when it comes to children of priests, the fruit of the act is a child, which can never be viewed as "lamentable" since such an outlook would be intrinsically contrary to the nature of the Catholic Church.

Thus, the Church is caught, do they condemn the "lamentable" act or outwardly praise the existence of these children?

Confidentiality agreements were sent from America, the Philippines and India. Secrets emerged about crimes committed against girls in mother and baby homes, in orphanages, from Ireland to Mexico.

The connection between ephebophilia, which is a sexual preference for adolescents, sexual abuse of minors, children of priests and religious and illegal adoptions became apparent, meaning scandals that emerged in the church incrementally, globally, were interlinked and not separate.

Sadly, even priests insisting on abortions, forcing the mothers to abort the child conceived became known to Coping.

Children sold at the backs of cathedrals, DNA uncovering long-held family secrets once thought to be buried in the grave, all emerged from the clay ridden depths of historic and trusted concealment.

The church had to respond, but responses were often found to be inadequate or absent entirely.

The Vatican introduced new and improved laws concerning the protection of minors regarding the age of consent, but is it enough? I always found it curious that the age of consent law exists under Canon Law in a Church that promotes chastity and celibacy. Regardless, if a priest fathers a child with a girl under eighteen years of age, is this ethical, even where civil law age of consent allows this? Is such an act Catholic, particularly when the man is middle-aged? Is it ever moral or right for a middle-aged man to have intercourse with an eighteen-year-old girl, whether the said act is legal or not? If the girl in question were over sixteen but under eighteen years of age, canon law before 2001 would not consider sex with someone between sixteen and eighteen, a canonical crime regardless of morality because the age of consent pre-2001 was sixteen.

Consequently, in cases presented to Coping where middle-aged priests fathered children with young girls, in some cases, the mother was just sixteen years old. Coping reports such cases to police and the CDF.

A Vatican official responded.

> "If the allegation refers to misconduct that happened before 2001 and the victim was over 16, then CDF cannot deal with it as a canonical delict."

In what lifetime is it ever ok for a grown man to have sex with a sixteen-year-old girl? Why would we want this to be ok? One afternoon, it was poorly explained away in one Vatican meeting, which I did not agree with.

"In certain cultures, [the official confirmed] girls are considered women aged 14 years and above."

Why would we explain away intercourse with whom we now recognise and legally consider to be a minor? In such scenarios where priests have had sex with 16-year-old girls, once the act occurred before 2001, if there is no complaining witness to testify to consent or lack thereof, the action goes unpunished.

Thus, should one change the legal consequence of a canonical act retroactively, where a priest or religious remains in ministry today, who is suspected of what is now considered child abuse, and has evaded civil law?

What message is the Catholic Church as an institution sending if she refuses to investigate a priest or religious canonically, still in active ministry, alleged to have abused a minor in the past, particularly when her child is the living DNA proof?

If the Church's defence for this inaction is reliant on the fact that institutionally, they refuse to apply new laws retroactively, then the problem lies not in the new post-2001 law itself, but the application of said law and interpretation of canon law.

Interpretation and application are of laws are direct acts, morally speaking, with foreseeable consequences and guilt and onus attached. Thus, from a theological and moral perspective, the non-retroactive application of the church law, knowingly, in the case of an ephebophile, facilitates alleged risk. Thus, one shares the burden of guilt toward not protecting minors.

The nature of the 2001 *Sacramentum Sanctitatis Tutela* relating to the age of consent -as not *ex post facto*- in and of itself acts as a means of enabling of a risk to minors today owing to its non-retroactive nature; thus, interpretation of the document does precisely the opposite to zero-tolerance. It tolerates.

It accepts alleged rapists and offenders based on the dates of their alleged offences enabling continuance of their ministry.

To the rebuttal that it is not right to apply a law retroactively on principle, ought one not from a catholic perspective, first and foremost reflect on the suitability of directly enabling the ministry of a priest/religious who has had sex with an adolescent by not applying a law retroactively?

All of this church law, risk toward minors, pregnancies, mothers abandoned, children sold, confidentiality agreements, forced and illegal adoptions landed on one small desk to one therapist. Even state authorities were reluctant and hesitant to help Coping appropriately, however, they eventually did, to a limited degree, but the Irish government let Coping down and the issue of children of priests down, repeatedly. Coping could only rely on the church, and we needed guidance, formal guidance from within.

Geneva, Switzerland, the Vatican Nuncio had invited me to mass at his residence. We had lunch before he showed me plants, planted by the former Nuncio, who resided there some years previously, none other than Archbishop Diarmuid Martin of Dublin.

Strikingly, Archbishop Diarmuid Martin, was the master of ceremonies at the ordination of my father in Cloniffe College, in Dublin, in 1966.

In Geneva, I found myself sitting at a brilliantly polished table in with Archbishop Jurkovič, the Apostolic Nuncio, Vatican Ambassador, to the United Nations.

A thin, brown folder was passed to me containing a single document, across the vast, immaculately polished table.

Silence fell over the room as I examined the mysterious sheet that lay before me.

The wafer-thin folder contained one single page only.

Mysterious in its content, the room heaved with a silent expectation as I thumbed and scanned the page, reading what lay before me.

The document was a set of guidelines written and composed by the Vatican's Congregation for Clergy, in 2009, under the guidance of Pope Benedict XVI. The name of the document in Italian reads, *'Nota relative alla prassi della Congregazione per il Clero a proposito dei chierici con prole,'* or *Notes concerning the practice of the Congregation for the Clergy with regard to clerics with children.'* The Irish Bishops released their own guidelines on the issue of children of priests in August 2017, the 'Principles of Responsibility Regarding Priests who father Children while in Ministry.' (Irish Catholic Bishops Conference., 2017) Both documents are landmark and worthy of praise and study.

The Vatican guidelines were initially described as internal or secret but later released to me. They were brief, succinct and covered less than one page. However, after they were expanded and developed, they became more detailed as was required.

No mention of mandatory expulsion of priests and religious leaving ministry following knowledge of paternity was mentioned on any version of the Vatican document. This is why I was particularly excited by this document.

Application of guidelines should always be done with due care and attention being paid toward psychological transference.

> "Transference [is] the unconscious transfer of experience from one interpersonal context to another, i.e. the reliving of past interpersonal relationships in current situations, including therapies." (Bennett., 2011)

Consequently, clergy who meet with the children of the ordained within a pastoral context should be familiar with this phenomenon. Children of the ordained may unconsciously encounter the cleric offering pastoral care in a paternal manner. Thus, professional boundaries are increasingly important within the context of responding to children of the ordained, since difficulties may arise for the child if the cleric responding is unaware of this risk. Thus, any and all guidelines should be offered toward the child, whilst remaining conscious of this reality.

Returning to the guidelines themselves, what the guidelines assume (the *ad* hoc reality that priests/religious can remain in ministry having become a parent) is helpful.

Thus, parents could, in theory at least, be open about their paternity without fear of unemployment resulting. It took a few short years to have what was initially secret, to be released. I spoke the Holy See, following meetings, they agreed that the guidelines could be released. They were formally released in January 2020.

> "The guidelines provided on the website of Coping International, with the noted Addendum, continue to be an accurate reflection of the approach of the Holy See to this delicate question, as articulated by the Cardinal Prefect in his now-famous interview with *L'Osservatore Romano*. While [we] understand your desire for the

Congregation or the Holy See itself to disseminate the guidelines in a more official way, it should be noted that these guidelines do not constitute a hard and fast rule of law.

A broad publication of our guidelines by the competent ecclesiastical authority could give the impression that every instance of clerical paternity necessitates departure from ministry and the loss of the clerical state.

In practice, the guidelines are much more nuanced, leaving open various options to deal with individual cases according to the child-focused paradigm that has developed since the pontificate of Benedict XVI. In the judgment of this Dicastery, acknowledging that your publication is a reliable presentation, without promulgating the document directly, allows for the subtle discernment required in each instance." (Congregation for Clergy., 2020)

The keywords here are "subtle discernment required in each instance." This is the reason the guidelines were released in an expanded form, in the text entitled, '*For children of priests, the good of the child comes first*', an interview with Cardinal Stella, by Andrea Tornielli and not originally in a PDF form, or on a letter. After the guidelines became known, latterly published on Coping, I asked the Congregation for Clergy the following question.

> **Doyle**: "Am I right in saying, these current Vatican Guidelines were updated since 2017?"
>
> **Congregation for Clergy**: "In that the Guidelines are a working document, they continue to be revised, as evidenced in the interview given by His Eminence Beniamino Cardinal Stella, the Prefect of the Congregation, to Mr. Tornielli, on 27 February 2019, and published in the Italian version of the Osservatore Romano and available in English on the Vatican News Website."
>
> (Congregation for Clergy., 2020)

Thus, from that thin sheet of paper in Geneva, the Vatican Guidelines have matured considerably since I first encountered them in 2017. The reason for this revision and ongoing revision is simple enough. As more becomes known about this phenomenon, the guidelines must mature and grow accordingly. It is to be expected that the Vatican guidelines may continue to develop in the future as this issue becomes more widely addressed and appreciated.

The most recent and up to date version of the Vatican guidelines appear on Coping's website today where you can access them freely, approved by the Holy See.

The history of the guidelines is interesting and relate to Pope Benedict XVI.

In 2009, Cardinal Hummes occupied the office of Prefect of Congregation for Clergy then. Here, he describes the mindset of Pope Benedict XVI on the matter of the children of priests.

> "Being a priest's [child] in no way can mean a burden or demerit for the [child]. I defended this clearly when (2006-2010) I was Prefect of the Congregation for the Clergy in the Roman Curia, and Benedict XVI was the Pope. He agreed with me, and since then I have guided the bishops who came to Rome for their 'ad limina visit' and also visited the Congregation for the Clergy." (Cardinal Claudio Hummes, 2019)

Sitting in Geneva with the Archbishop, I was somewhat stunned that guidelines existed.

This meant that the Vatican knew of this issue and made that knowledge official. The Archbishop, that morning did go on the record which is possibly the first on the record statement by any Vatican official concerning children of priests and their welfare in history.

> **"Doyle:** 'Does the Holy Father [Pope Francis] understand the problem of mental health-related issues, relating to silence and children of ordained?'
>
> **+ Jurkovič:** 'Yes, the Holy Father does understand this problem. There exists a responsibility on behalf of the Catholic Church. Moreover, the priest who fathers a child has more than a financial responsibility, not forsaking the latter, but a relationship of 'being close' to his child.'
>
> **Doyle:** 'What does the Pope intend on doing to ensure kids are cared for considering the above-mentioned problem relating to mental health?'
>
> **+ Jurkovič:** 'A holistic approach is required toward this issue. Quality of life is important.'
>
> **Doyle:** 'Is it possible for the Holy See to state something along the lines, regarding the issue pertaining to children

of ordained, "be not afraid to approach your Bishop / Religious Superior if you are the child of a priest or mother of the child of an ordained person?"

+ Jurkovič: 'Yes, this is possible.'

Doyle: 'Is the issue regarding children of ordained a child protection issue for the entire Catholic Church?'

+ Jurkovič: 'Yes, absolutely.'

Doyle: 'Do numbers matter relating to [the] quantity of children of ordained? Secondly, would a smaller number of children of ordained persons in any way lessen the gravity of the situation?'

+ Jurkovič: 'Numbers are important from a statistical perspective. However, from a Church perspective, no, numbers in no way lessen the gravity of the situation.'

Doyle: 'When is the report in reply to the 2014 Concluding Recommendations, on behalf of the Holy See expected and will it include / reference children of ordained?'

+ Jurkovič: 'The report is being worked on as we speak.'

The Archbishop continued to assert the importance of

working groups such as Coping, and research completed by same, to assist the Catholic Church so [that] she may grow in knowledge." (Coping International, 2017)

From the streets of North County Dublin to Geneva and the steps of the Vatican, a journey initiated by one man, would be followed and mimicked by many more to come. As hurt and pain began to ebb from the closed minds and mouths of children of the ordained globally, a resolution had to be fostered and disseminated.

A psychosocial battle had begun on the streets of Dublin and Boston, New York and Rome making its way inside the Vatican, who would respond with the admittance of knowledge of the issue and guidelines, composed during one of the most influential papacies of recent times.

Assumed non-existence of children of priests was being defeated, beaten, thus authenticating the issues and existences of the children of the ordained.

From that thin sheet of paper that slipped across the tiled kitchen floor in county Longford to an equally thin layer, slid across an ornate table in Geneva, Switzerland; the key to Coping's success lay in acknowledging deliberate non-acknowledgement of this issue.

This was achieved by creating a space for the children of the ordained, where their problems became visible, using Catholic teaching. What eventually became visible was a global phenomenon that had been hidden for centuries.

Now that the world had seen us, the secret children of priests, understanding their plight, understanding their suffering would prove crucial to fostering a responsible global response.

The socially engrained silence that surrounded this issue was both deliberate and conscious. The word *Silentium* in Latin refers to silence, stillness, or inaction.

> I refer to the systemic silencing of the child of a priest or religious regarding their paternity as '*Silentium.*'

Sadly, another effect of *Silentium* is how it has a residual impact directly upon partners and families of the child of the ordained. The latter (partner) is often in a warped way, sucked into this perverse world of secrecy and deception and all that it entails, unfairly so.

The residue of *Silentium* or 'Residual *Silentium*' infuses the relationship that the priest's child engages in, triggering difficulties, like an infection, promoting behaviours beyond what might be considered normal, affecting the third party.

This is why boundaries are significant for children of the ordained.

In the situation where a man or woman who is the son or daughter of a priest are burdened with personal and social difficulties, it may be the case that their adopted behaviours, central to sustaining *Silentium* that they habituated early in life, distracting them, are categorically foreign to what is commonly accepted as normal behaviour. Consequently, this affects their partner and relationship adversely.

Residual *Silentium* may be present even when and where the children of priests or religious outwardly prefer secrecy surrounding their identity. Inwardly, tension may subsist fostering unconscious anxiety, affecting psychological integration, consequently, affecting personal relationships, partners and friends. This is unfair to these people.

Silentium is a cancerous fruit that erodes the wellbeing of an endless sea of suffering children and has done for centuries. *Silentium* is a gateway where wilful, adult-centered sacrifice becomes psychological and emotional child abuse.

However, the voices of the children of the ordained could now be heard above the clericalist fist that muted them for centuries, now they and their families had a light, and into the light of openness, we went, with force.

Chapter Two.

Out of Darkness.

Opening the door to my small office each morning, I am never sure what is about to greet me. I enjoy routine, prayer, coffee, dogs, quietude.

After I feed my dogs and make a coffee, my computer is turned on.

Overnight and daily, people continue to come to Coping, unique visitors from across the globe, children of the ordained and religious, not forsaking priests, religious. All are part of secret families that history and society pretended it knew nothing of, least in the quantities they are presenting and reproducing today. Each DNA test, each email, each letter, phone call, every unique visitor from the 175 countries presenting to Coping over the past number of years, represents a human being.

These unknown persons all carry a story within them, and within that story is pain, pain that is new to the world, begging to be let out, to heal. However, they do not know where to turn.

"I thought I was the only one" is a phrase I heard almost every day. The cruelty that spills from these stories that appear via letter, email and telephone is unimaginable.

In my quiet office as my dogs' sleep, I read with horror, the trauma that people have suffered and continue to suffer, and all in the name of alleged holiness.

In this, holiness is feigned, and the child disrespected.

Sometimes I play music, music that soothes the Coping office, a room that heaves with global sadness and anxiety, a pressure that belongs to people I have never met and most I never will.

As sunlight strives to melt the moist fog sleeping over Irish fields where in my father lies, my mind ruminates the many internal, lonely rooms that I wandered, in my heart and mind, for years, alone, searching and thinking, believing something was wrong, yet not knowing what exactly?

I use music, often Ludovico Einaudi or Hayley Westenra to assist in calming what could be a burdensome environment, heaving with global pain and anxieties.

I remember Barbara Dever, the Mezzo-soprano who honoured JJ by singing Verdi's Requiem with the Israel Philharmonic in July 1995, weeks after he had died. She dedicated her performance to his memory. As hearts in Jerusalem soared bittersweetly, lifted by Barbara's heartfelt dedication, one little boy with a broken heart, rode a blue bike, lovingly bought by a priest, every day to a graveyard, with my dog running beside me.

I believe the dog that JJ had bought me understood better what had happened than most others.

As Barbara's voice rose into the night sky over Jerusalem, a little voice softly and mutedly, whispered into clouds over Ireland, for fear other visitors in the graveyard, might hear my confused, tear-filled prayers.

I whispered to the small wooden cross that marked his final resting spot, telling him how much I missed him.

As Barbara Dever's awestruck audience wiped their tears of emotional relief in Jerusalem, I wiped mine, alone, by that small, wooden cross beneath the chorus of the birds, my constant audience.

I told JJ what had happened that day, what I hoped might happen. Spot, my dog, rested his small, black nose in the now sinking clay, silently burying my heart, deep within the progressive seasons. When asked if I spoke to JJ when I visited the graveyard, an old diary entry reveals my answer, the innocent words belonging to a twelve-year-old boy, tormented by hidden grief that lay entombed in silence and confusion.

> "No, I just water the flowers there, but I talk to JJ in the sky. JJ is not in the graveyard. How could I sleep in my nice warm bed at night if JJ was in the graveyard? Thank God, he is in heaven."

Confusion, death, expectancy and compliance silenced me, and I didn't even know it. I had no idea, consciously, that I was sitting at the grave of my beloved father. Though, my heart was deeply confused and would remain so for almost two decades and all for the preservation of peace.

How I wish I could have been in Jerusalem to ease my tears, to rest my spirit upon the chorus, that July of 1995.

However, my place was by his grave, silent and still as the priest that lay buried by his grieving parishioners beneath the clay.

Dew slid off the gentle blades of grass, as the fields wept in veiled silence with me. The wind touched and eased my laboured breath as I tried in vain to pray and breathe. Though the grave subsided as did my grief, somehow heartache remained, interred within me, still and mute as death itself, awaiting an unexpected resurrection.

There is nothing holy or sanctified about *Silentium*, the deliberate silencing of the child of a priest/religious. The palpable hypocrisy that rests itself upon the softened head of a child is as shrewd as it is dangerous. Silencing a child denatures the child organically, and this silencing is doubly cruel since it is habitually disguised as the moral thing to do to avoid shame, scandal, and outrage.

What effect has *Silentium* upon a child?

Is *Silentium* different from silencing a child whose father is not a priest, whose family prefer to keep the paternity under wraps? This question was asked of me in the Vatican some years ago.

I found myself seated at an extraordinarily large table, with a sheen that was reminiscent of the table in Geneva when I first saw the Vatican Guidelines.

I somehow always find myself seated at large tables in Rome, with truly little in front of me other than water and hope.

"Why pick on priests' kids?" the Vatican prelate curtly queried. It was a test to see if I understood the nuances specific to this issue. I sat in stilled silence as I considered my response in an office at the end of *Via Della Conciliazione* in Rome.

> "If a doctor fathers a child with a nurse out of wedlock, I very much doubt the respective department of health would fuss about the status of the child, and *that* is the difference", I confidently asserted.

The entire tone in the room changed afterwards. It was as if a window was opened and we engaged on a much more fundamental level. The priest opened up telling me about a priest he knows in Peru who has a child, who nobody seems to know about, even going so far as to tell me his name.

His openness surprised me and said to me that much is known, but extraordinarily little is said. To me, this was further evidence of the blatant non-acknowledgement of these children.

The silence that surrounds the children of priests is linked with their mental health. *Silentium* is institutional and systemic, it is historic and cunning, for it is disguised as privacy, as what is right for the child, to avert unwanted media intrusion. However, if all the priest's children in the world stood up and we were all counted, past, present and future, there would scarcely be enough cameras in the world to photograph us all, nor would there be a need to, for we would lose our uniqueness as children of priests. We would just be known as children!

If all the children of the ordained and religious were cared for as requested by the United Nations in 2014, the click of the journalist's camera would fade away as it slowly became accepted that the priest's child is no different to the doctor and nurse's child. But it is the silence surrounding this issue that fuels the fascination on this topic, which is linked with mothers and fathers fearing exposure.

Silentium remains a reality for all children of priests globally. *Silentium* reverses the natural order of things, the child becomes the guardian of a perverse silence, nurturing it with astute paranoia and fear during their lifetime.

I speak with a woman in her sixties regularly, a client who is the daughter of an Irish priest. Though she was born out of love, her father and mother are long dead, and she was adopted. When I broach the topic of openness, she shudders, citing her friends who would talk and be "shocked saying, 'isn't it awful and terrible.' I'd be the talk of the town." Here we see a woman crippled by fear and paranoia, a paranoia that is rooted in causing scandal, yet the protagonists are all dead. Still, the secret remains intergenerationally. In this, the adopted child, now a woman, is conditioned by silence and the expectation to be obedient and docile to a menacing silence for her entire life, wrongly so.

I imagine her flour-covered fingers kneading the dough on her country table, humming, and saying that all is well, radio plays in vain trying to drown out all the things in her head. Internally, in her hidden world, this countrywoman remains in a cavern of fear trembling with aggravation and paranoia, beneath the shadow of *Silentium*.

Conditional parenting is central to *Silentium*, and the two go hand in hand. The child's needs are met based on obedience to a heaving burden of silence that consumes their world.

Frozen within a world of isolation and seclusion, the child becomes separated from what other children might consider as being normal. What remains unique to the children of the ordained is the instilled belief that, if the child opens their mouth about their priestly heritage, society itself would be unpleasantly affected. In contrast, a child fathered by a married man, for instance, might foster idle gossip briefly, before the story would fade away.

The child of the priest was, is and remains to be the evidence that chastity and indeed celibacy (in the case where priests marry the mother in civil ceremonies to legitimise the child, particularly in developing cultures) is broken, abandoned and only partially maintained globally.

This is the way it has always been. Former Popes were allegedly the children of Popes, including Pope John XI (Pontificate ended

936), was allegedly the son of Pope Sergius III, and Pope Silverius (Pontificate ended 537), son of Pope Hormisdas, as noted on the website of the Holy See. (Cholij, n.d.)

However, institutional fear reigns, and it is this fear, the fear of the tradition of celibacy being overwhelmed by clerical indiscretion, that wrongly necessitates *Silentium* alongside conditional parenting.

This is not Catholic and completely disingenuous to any spiritual fruit afforded by authentic celibacy. If chaste celibacy's authenticity must be propped up by the sealed lips of the children of the ordained, then its apparent lack of humility impinges any integrity it lays claim to. Franco Ferrarotti notes,

> "children of sin, [are] destined, for their existence and independently of their will, to demonstrate the finitude and the limits of even the most sublime vocation. The children of priests are in fact the living proof of human sinfulness and at the same time the testimony of a biblical promise that has not been kept." (Ferrarotti, 2020)

Ferrarotti's use of the term "children of sin" might seem harsh. However, it reminds us of Pope Saint Paul VI, who cited "lamentable defection" in 1967 referring to clergy who stray from their promises and vows. The focus should always be on the child, and no child should be characterised or branded by their conception.

As a consequence of *Silentium*, basic needs such as the need for food, a home, and education seemingly remains entirely contingent upon a child's ability to keep quiet about something so natural, as well as their capacity to deceive and be deceived.

This is where coercive control manipulates and ransoms basic needs against the need for transparency, freedom and honesty, but this is done so subtly and shrewdly and over time.

Thus, their physical needs are ransomed against their psychological and emotional needs. This is wrong and indicates the presence of conditional parenting.

Children of the priests' needs are met on the condition that they remain obedient and docile to the secrecy that lords over their very existence from conception to death. This is an anti-pro-life sentiment.

Prolonged exposure to conditional parenting equally has maladaptive effects in the long term. Indeed, it takes a village to raise a child, but if that child is made unwelcome in that same village, a community that stigmatises may become a baying mob in the mind of the child, who is crippled with paranoia and fear as a result.

The internalised anxiety that results from not being allowed to talk about one's identity, fear of rejection or feeling intimidated distracts the child and disrupts their development. The child may feel somebody knows about who they are, which they believe may have catastrophic consequences. This promotes massive amounts of internal pressure and paranoia. Prolonged anxiety may emerge as anger, uncontrollable anger, unreasonableness, social awkwardness, even irrationality who no apparent source.

Children of priests and religious that I speak with regularly, in my small dog-friendly office, with habitual coffee cup nestled beneath the monitors, don't know, down their street, in their town, in their country are more hidden children.

The "I'm the only one mentality", referring children who believe they are the only priest's child in the world is so strong, it convinces people almost beyond belief, that they are the only one. Nothing could be further from the truth.

At my small desk, pc mouse in hand, somewhat warm, as it rests by my perpetual coffee mug, people speak to me from countries, some of which I never knew existed.

They tell of clerical and religious paternity, social isolation, poverty, and extreme marginalisation and how none of it was ever acknowledged, a cruel existence, characterised by non-acknowledgement.

I have heard of devastating stories where houses were firebombed following a radio broadcast where it became known that a priest had fathered children.

Then there are the stories of rape, rape of minors, ephebophilia, where a girl becomes pregnant. If she is from a developing country, she faces ostracism. Or the young woman faced with walking hundreds of miles out of her home country, sleeping in bus shelters, because she had disgraced herself by becoming a mother to priests' children. Or the religious sisters, raped and impregnated, with little economic opportunity, resorting to prostitution to feed themselves. The man who was forced out of his country and sent to Australia so that the priest could hide his shame, or the priest in Germany who in 2020, called the pregnant woman who he impregnated "evil" because she would not abort the child. He could not control the child if they lived, and besides, he already had one that he left behind in Africa.

One must not forget the cardinal who has children bemused at their audacity, after all, he did educate them, even though he silenced them. Or the priest's child in India who advises of a process of not teaching children of the ordained in primary school, since then, their compliance with secrecy is more likely owing to illiteracy and lacking primary education.

Regarding this alleged process, I emailed Cardinal Oswald Gracias. I asked him the following question.

> "The child of a Catholic Bishop in India informs me that there exists a practise in India of not educating children born to priests and religious, thereby lessening the likelihood of said children ever revealing details about their paternity and home life as they are consequently likely to exist in a dependent state with less confidence."

His Eminence replied,

> "I know your passion for the Cause. But the assertion you make about a practice in India is just absurd. I know of no such cases." (Gracias., 2020)

I respect Cardinal Gracias. He has always been kind to me. However, poor schooling is a consequence of economic deprivation, which itself is a consequence of not putting children first, ahead of adult's rights, concerning children of the ordained inside as well as outside of India. Thus, inadequate schooling is a foreseeable consequence of deficient supports which is a fruit of *Silentium*.

Then there was the priest in Mexico who rapes girls in an orphanage, who is alleged to have dozens of children. Or the priest in the States, whose child heard of his death on a newspaper and to this day is fighting to gain access to the States so she can say goodbye to the man she called father, years after his death. The boy in the Philippines who wrote a letter to the pope, who wonders why his father no longer works and is sad because he thinks his father does not like him. The plight of grandchildren must not be overlooked. They inherit a burden laid on top of their parents by the Catholic Church and society and are forced to comply with irrational and learned behaviours their parents complied with as children, all to protect the adults concerned. The plight of grandchildren is reminiscent of Residual *Silentium*.

And yet, it is so common, so historic, so much a part of our culture, still, this phenomenon is veiled behind the seemingly impenetrable and ancient curtains of silence, denial, and rejection, that is, *Silentium*.

The children of priests, like the images of children in developing countries carrying water on their head, unmerciful distances, are expected to say "ok" over and over, to such a menacing wolf in sheep's clothing, *Silentium* itself disguised as privacy.

However, one thing is for sure, privacy minus choice equates abuse. If it were really about privacy, the man or woman, priest or religious would have an option of remaining or leaving, and that choice would not be rhetorical but actual.

It would not be laden with apology and regret, nor the words "lamentable defection."

Neither would the female religious have to leave her job, but she would be thanked for her service if she left, the same with the priest, and both would be left in a position of employment. However, it is easier to say, "he left to care for his child."

It sounds good but has little if any meaning.

How can we expect a child to understand this reality?

How do you explain it?

The other side of the coin is those who do not tell of the child's existence, silencing them. Neither scenario is desirable.

The Irish Department of Children and Youth Affairs agree,

> "'premature imposition of responsibility on [a] child [to] [...] understand something or to behave and control himself or herself in a certain way" (DCYA, 2011.) [is an indicator of] emotional abuse."

To expect that a child has the wherewithal to psychologically support themselves under such a burden of pressure from infancy into adulthood, is like attaching a cement block to their head and simultaneously anticipating natural growth.

What is incredible and curious in equal measure is making contingent, a child supporting the weight of *Silentium* alongside the expectation that natural, healthy development will inevitably result *owing* to the presence of *Silentium* not despite its presence. It is ludicrous to expect that a child can healthily develop in such a denaturing and stifling environment, one that is laden with secrecy, emotional abuse, and conditional parenting. Such an expectation is as ludicrous as anticipating that all priests and religious will never become parents. It is as ridiculous as responding to said paternity with automatic and accelerated departure from ministry, even when the said parent does not wish to marry, forcing unemployment, and in some cases, resultant homelessness. It is as ludicrous as the hypocrisy of any industry in the world, who promote care, systemically responding to paternity with automatic unemployment.

The Catholic Church would rightly be the first in line to confirm that mandatory involuntary unemployment owing to paternity is contrary to the dignity of the child and their family.

The anxiety that emanates from the pressure of conditional parenting is as palpable as it is gradual, as the child contorts emotionally and psychologically around the superfluous and extraneous demands imposed upon them by mother, father, and

Church. The child's natural rights are continuously accompanied by absolute compliance with secrecy.

The Australian National Catholic Safeguarding Standards defines psychological abuse as follows:

> "a failure to provide adequate non-physical nurture or emotional availability. Psychologically abusive behaviours include *rejecting*, ignoring, isolating, terrorising, corrupting, verbal abuse and belittlement." (Catholic Professional Standards Ltd. , 2019)

However, a further difficulty arises in the fact that the child may grow accustomed to the maladaptive patterns in the home that are fostered and nurtured by *Silentium*. These are processes that protect the adult, so the adult/child protection relationship is reversed. Whilst the child outwardly complies and may appear docile in the face of being silenced, inwardly *Silentium* negates natural inclinations. Though the child resists being silenced inwardly, he or she cannot verbalise this rejection of *Silentium* for there exists no precursor for such rejection.

This inward negative effect, if it cannot be verbalised or understood fully by the child, may emanate differently.

It may come out via unruly or disruptive behaviour, for instance, psychosomatically.

The unsociability displayed by the child consequently may reduce the likelihood of the biological parents ever freeing the child from the secrecy surrounding their paternity, assuming such disclosure would make things worse not improve the child's overall health.

The parents wrongly assume that allowing the child to be utterly open concerning their paternity would worsen the child's behaviour and conduct. Consequently, a vicious cycle ensues. *Silentium* promotes negative mental health, which lessens the likelihood of *Silentium* ever being removed from the child's life and existence.

This results in chronic internal cyclical anxiety, which affects the child is so many ways, education, housing, relationships, amid a myriad of aspects of their lives destroyed by lack of focus, distractedness, anxiety, and depression.

The source of all this pain, of being silenced, not knowing or possessing uncertain knowledge about paternity, *Silentium*, is erroneously perceived as the appropriate remedy for the wound that the children of priests' experience.

Conversely, it is the catalyst of child-centred pain, coercive control and psychological and emotional abuse. Thus, cyclical anxiety.

Like acid reflux, anxiety will always make itself known.

Silentium is wrongly believed to be a protection mechanism that guards the child when, in fact, it is the cause of much of the child's anxiety, as it is unnatural to the child. However, the child is unlikely to wake up one day announcing,

> "I am anxious and afraid because I can't say that the priest is my daddy and being able to say that will fix all my woes, *phew* ... that's a relief."

When the child reaches a mature age, they will likely have adapted and grown accustomed to the expectations placed upon them by parents, church and to a lesser extent, society, and social custom.

They will have ritualised certain practises or social situations, mastering them, so as not to reveal the long-held family secret. They may be forced to lie and may also be adept at this, which is a ruthless skill to foster in any child. However, whilst they are outwardly focused on mastery of social events and non-disclosure of paternity in any number of social scenarios, they disregard their emotional and psychological well-being neglected by all the manipulation in their life. When one's immediate, physical and shelter needs, are believed to be contingent upon maintenance of secrecy surrounding one's identity, psychological needs are rarely if ever, prioritised. One client of Coping describes her inner world when she finally reconnected with that silenced, gagged inner child long sought to be buried by people with evil intent. The following are her own words reprinted as per her request to make know the effect of *Silentium*

> "I saw a young girl strapped to a medical restraint, arms and legs bound with leather straps, at a 45-degree angle (as if on display) in a blue-tiled and depressingly gloomy room. Alone, she was screaming at pitch point, red in the face, veins bursting, head outstretched. She could feel the physical force of her desire for freedom manifesting itself. This force or push made even more real, her emotional pain, authenticating it. Outside (she is on the inside of me),

I remain completely disassociated from her (the girl on the bed). The two (adult and inner child) remain at odds, as if twins at birth, separated. She screamed to the point that I could feel the caress of her tiny tear on my cheek through the ice-stained circumference that was my outer being. Then, our tear -as I sat in stilled silence, trembling- pushed through, though just a few, and then, it was gone."

The scariest and loneliest thing about this is this person absolutely and unequivocally detached from this inward reality soon after, regaining a seemingly healthy outward composure that could grace even the most glamourous of social situations. She was chronically manipulated from birth by her mother.

She became the guardian of a priest's secret and her mother's secret. It was as if she was moulded to portray what the mother wanted, which could never be discerned as her mother was a chronic narcissist, so the daughter began to self-sabotage.

Her identity was buried beneath custom and the social tradition of the purported non-existence of children of priests. Buried at birth beneath clay of determined ignorance, her wellbeing became entombed, walled in by silence that has circumnavigated the institutional Church, globally, historically, and unendingly, for centuries, always masked as the right thing to do.

The mother's fear impacted her child. *Silentium* penetrated the domestic environment of the child to the point where it alongside its effect was normalised. Consequently, when natural curiosities raised their heads as she matured, they were quickly tidied away. She confirmed that she was told repeatedly, "call him father, like everyone else" referring to her biological father.

Her training remained and like a diligent soldier.

However, despite breaking down in front of me, her social and psychological makeup was applied, smile reattached, and child buried deep in the subconscious, psychological caverns that she had foraged out during her childhood. She made room to escape in these small rooms in her head, places constructed by distraction and noise, to escape the hell of being abused.

She lost almost all, if not all, of her ability to feel or connect emotionally. Irish Psychotherapist, Patricia O'Reilly notes,

> "in the first trimester in the womb, humans encounter the origins of the main personality disorders and

psychosomatic stress conditions that affect us throughout our lives." (O'Reilly, 2020)

Collectively speaking, it is the experience and witness of Coping, while the priest's child is busily monitoring the everydayness of maintaining the secrecy that they have inherited, inside, their emotional and psychological health deteriorates rapidly.

In place of peace and happiness are anxiety and nervousness.

This anxiety, like all things, must come out, and consequently, it manifests psychosomatically or via disruptive behaviour.

The psychosocial environment wherein the family live may be hostile to the reality of priestly paternity.

Thus, to avoid external conflict, the small family unit remains quiet, and the pregnancy is hidden, or the biological father is named as another man.

However, whether the biological father's identity is known about or not, the internal fear within the mother, her guilt, possible feelings of shame for deceiving her child and other people affect her, negatively and thus her child. The more she conceals these feelings, the more they are likely to overwhelm her eventually and her child.

"There is now considerable evidence that the mother's emotional state during pregnancy can affect the development of her baby's brain. This is because of 'foetal programming', where a changing environment in the womb through different sensitive periods can alter the development of the foetus. This then goes on to affect the child in the longer term and into adulthood." (Kahn, 2013)

Thus, one might draw a link between *Silentium* and foetal programming', negatively affecting the child.

It is this affected behaviour (within the mother) over time, that affects her child.

Communication between the two is stunted by the presence of secrecy between the two. The child remains to be a visible manifestation of her secret. She may feel that she needs to keep the secret until her death locked up, so too the child, locked within her secret. Each day she looks at the priest's child, each time she passes a Church or meets a priest, she is reminded of that silent, internally abiding fear within her, a reality she pretends, does not exist. She, as the mother, knows the full truth about the child's paternity, who in turn may not know about their priestly fatherhood.

This may seem like the best thing, but it is not always effective. Many children from a young age, via the visible pressure present within the home, suspect something is wrong. As they mature, they recognise incrementally that this pressure is somehow linked to them.

The child of the priest grows suspicious over time since no secret is absolute. I have seen this process occur time and time again, with people that have presented to Coping. The mother's fear of the paternity being discovered promotes anxiety within her. Anxiety and fear encourage distractedness, absent-mindedness, or preoccupation on behalf of the mother. It is the disharmony that surrounds the mother where suspicion grows on behalf of the child. This encourages the child to seek out the root of this prolonged disharmony.

A 2005 commission concerning the topic of assisted reproduction notes as follows.

"Secrecy may exacerbate disharmony rather than promote family relationships, as the child overhears partial allusions to his [or her] conception and hears half-truths and evasions from his parents in reply." (Report of the Commission on Assisted Human Reproduction., 2005)

Therefore, even where direct knowledge of paternity is absent, the truth seeps through the crack of deception over time fostering suspicion which seeks an answer.

It is typical for the child of a priest to tell the story that the priest who fathered them was referred to as an uncle, or in my case, my Godfather.

Indeed, I was interested in the bond I shared with my Godfather. Whilst I relished it and loved our relationship, with an intensity like no other, it confused me simultaneously.

Why did this priest mean so much to me, and why did I mean so much to him? Nobody else seemed to matter that much to him, and he was different with me than he was with others? We had our private communication.

We customarily put our thumb up toward one another, indicating being "best buds." He smiled so lovingly at me, and we spoke daily. Whilst I willingly accepted this happiness, it similarly made no sense? It became increasingly difficult when he died, as the grief customarily associated with a boy who is not a son did not match that which I felt internally.

So, I like the children conceived via assisted reproduction, I too recognised a level of internal disharmony which promoted curiosity.

Maternal disharmony unwittingly nurtures child-centred suspicion incrementally. Very often for the priest's child, their suspicion cannot be verbalised as the child has neither the maturity nor vocabulary to express the confusion.

However, it will grow to the point where the child has sufficient maturity and a language to match, and this is how secrets get outed, initially via intuition and instinct and finally via questioning and eventually suspicions are confirmed via home DNA testing.

You must remember, he or she is the child of the one imposing the secret and thus will have inherited similar behaviour patterns, looks, and personal traits, that signify more than an ordinary friendship existing between the adult and child.

These cues point toward a hidden reality when the child is allegedly unaware of their paternity.

Over time, the child may notice subtle differences that appear when compared with his or her friend's families, who do not display such awkward behaviours.

What may stand out are small perceptible differences in how the mother acts or talks about the Catholic Church. If the priest remains in the life of the mother as is often the case to ensure obedience to *Silentium*, the child may notice differences in how she acts toward him (negatively or positively), as opposed to her reactions toward other priests and other people.

Social norms incrementally and subtly are affected, and the child perceives and accumulates this as a body of knowledge, encouraging curiosity.

Consequently, *Silentium* can indirectly affect a child, even when they have not been directly told about their priestly paternity, they may realise it over time, despite best efforts to the contrary by the adults concerned.

I speak to children daily, all of whom are now adults, with noted exceptions where a minor would accompany the mother in full knowledge of their clerical paternity.

I see commonalities that are not culturally specific. There exists a misguided belief that there is a problem with multitudes of children of priests in Africa, suggesting that there exists no similar problem of equal magnitude in developing countries. There is a strange belief or tendency to commonly associate the phenomenon of children of priests alongside developing cultures only.

This assumption is wrong and misleading. There are children of priests globally.

It is a phenomenon that is not contingent upon economics.

Whilst, in South Africa there have been more than 3,500 hits on Coping and growing, not to mention regular traffic from the Democratic Republic of the Congo, Kenya, Uganda, South Sudan to name but a few. Equally, it is developed countries where we see the most significant volume of traffic. What Coping has shown is that this is a global phenomenon that cannot be curbed; it can only be veiled and concealed, wrongly so. No child should be hidden.

The commonalities displayed by almost all secret children of priests is a desire for freedom.

The child wishes to be freed from the shackles that have enslaved them, trapping them within a confusing maze of darkness uncommon to childhood, manipulated continuously by conditional parenting, *Silentium* and fear.

Thus, *Silentium* is a clericalist virus that adapts to culture and context and is a form of psychological and emotional slavery.

Many are so relieved to express what they believe is so unique that words could scarcely describe the pain they feel.

Children of priests and religious who suffer beneath the heaving social burden become unburdened when they realise, they are indeed not the only one, when they speak to one another, they feel relief and great joy.

What could be viewed negatively about this?

The persistence of the belief that ignorance is bliss, and it is ok to not tell the child about their paternity probably never envisages a

DNA test quickly unearthing truth from the inside cheek of the child's mouth years later.

Among the most famous of such cases proving priestly fatherhood was that of the case of Mr Jim Graham, from the USA who exhumed his late father to confirm paternity, from his grave. Jim, a dear friend, set a precedent, a historical one, and for this, he should be commended.

In 1964, a term, genealogical bewilderment was coined. The term first appeared in 1952 when "an apparently large number of adopted children had been referred to the child guidance clinic [...]." (Sants., 1964)

> "A genealogically bewildered child is one who either has no knowledge of his natural parents or only uncertain knowledge of them. The resulting state of confusion and uncertainty [...] fundamentally undermines his security and thus affects his mental health." (Sants., 1964)

For the child of a priest, genealogical bewilderment as a source of anxiety may propel them to find out a concealed truth, either overtime or via DNA testing.

Suspicion, anxiety, and a sense of bewilderment are not only confusing for the child, but also it is linked with anger, on behalf of the child, hearkening the unruly behaviour mentioned previously.

The consequences of denied heritage are multitudinous and intergenerational. The individual concerned is denied a mirror image of themselves in present-day living relatives and stories surrounding their ancestors which may mirror a part of their existence.

They are denied intergenerational confirmation of traits or characteristics or resemblances which promote safety and inclusion.

Concealing heritage feeds secrecy. It is this very secrecy which fosters neglect, for the deepest part of the self remains unauthenticated and invalidated.

The oldest case of intergenerational abuse filtering down through family generations, that has presented to Coping, reaches back to 1936.

In 1936, a priest fathered a daughter in the United States.

Today, twelve of her offspring from the same family are all in counselling.

The great-grandchild of the woman fathered by the priest spoke about her father to me. He grew up nurtured by the woman who had to navigate her life around an enormous secret.

Stories like this arrive on our desk daily and show no signs of abating.

The Catholic Church had and still has a substantial impact on the social and professional life of Catholic communities. Thus, the priest's daughter was wrongly led to believe that she would undermine all that was good, wholesome, and decent within that community. She absorbed this belief and grew to know it as truth.

"Forgive us for being alive", the words of UK based Artist, Mr John Anderson, a friend, and son of a French Catholic priest, taken from his poem, *Child of God.*

John Anderson bittersweetly captures the sense of grief together with regret and shame, present in the children of the ordained globally.

This ball of enmeshed confusion that exists in the vulnerable mind of the child of the ordained is penned by a historic and ancient process of the Catholic Church - pretending their priests and religious do not have children.

Secretly, this false belief is inscribed upon the hearts and minds of their vulnerable children, intergenerationally. It silences them, betraying not only children but the goodness of the priesthood itself.

This is not what Christ intended. This is man's intention masked as God's will.

What is sad, or at least should be, for any discerning Catholic, is that these social impediments that contradict natural law.

These menacing and fearful, unwritten laws of oppression that denature the children of the ordained globally, daily, are enabled and enacted so that the priest and religious may continue unchallenged, preaching the word of God.

What is the point of that?

Perhaps that is the greatest sin, to use one's desire to promote God's word, as a catalyst to psychologically annihilate God's creation, the child of God systemically.

The certainty and future inevitability of the existence of the children of the ordained should be sufficient to elicit a better response by the institutional Church than one of non-acknowledgement, conditional parenting, silencing, the premature imposition of responsibility upon a child and neglect.

My desk is laden with trauma, and my dogs are still asleep. Morning stretches out across the green, wet fields.

Cattle appear as prominent as daisies in the distance. My coffee stills me, within the moment as barks in the distance tell me that I must abandon the trauma that has greeted me in the fresh and crisp autumn morning, if only for a little while and find my dogs. I walk away, but I know it will be there waiting for me, breathing, waiting, hiding and disguising so many vulnerable, innocent children, a problem that won't stop, until priests can be parents openly.

As the barks continue, a bird escapes the clutches of a branch waving in the wind.

I will finish and relish my coffee, then return to step back inside this hidden world, specially sculpted with non-acknowledgement and finished with a thick veneer of imposed silence, a world that seeks only to engulf, control, and conceal.

Trauma darkly gifts the children of the ordained one thing. Now the priestly sacrifice no longer belongs to our fathers' alone, it belongs to us, the children of the ordained who are anointed with suffering.

We exist in a confusing world of silence that we instinctually know will do us only harm and no good at all.

A poem from my father's collection, entitled 'My World', printed overleaf acknowledges the segregated world of priest-fathers, a world often characterised by loneliness.

He waited for "one tiny footstep, a face […] to enter [his] world."

JJ loved me, and I loved him.

I was due to spend the evening with him that Sunday in late July, games, fun, enjoyment. JJ and I had planned to go to America to visit with family when I turned fourteen.

I am informed that this was when he was going to tell me. That day never arrived, unfortunately.

JJ died, leaving me in this world, feeling strangely alone. I remained without his care and attention. This world was safe with him. However, in his absence, it was devoid of any semblance of certainty, because an unexpected death broke our seemingly inseparable bond, and no one could replace him in my heart.

I did not know how to navigate this dark clerical world that linked me with the Roman Catholic Church.

Every collar I saw, he was not behind it.

So, I stayed close to the Church, for it was all I knew.

They had no blueprint for people like me who meandered this secret clerical world, and I had no words to explain my grief, until now. Thus, my path, so no other child will be muted by expectation, cruelty and child abuse.

Today, my footstep alights upon another door than the small step of the parochial house where my late father lived, the Vatican.

I do this, so children like my inner child may find a way out of the imposed darkness, alive and well, illuminated by 'Kaslyn's lamp.'

Only truth will set the church and her children free, truth, freeing us from the intergenerational psychological prison woven by history, greed and selfishness so cruelly disguised as the right thing to do.

MY WORLD

Cars come and go,

start and fade away

and I sit here alone

and wait.

Wait for one special sound,
one tiny footstep,

a face in the doorway.
Enter my world.

Chapter Three.

The Moral Argument falls Apart.

It is a curious thing, the strength of what I call, the Moral Argument, the unceasing and unyielding claim that a priest or religious must leave the ministry, in every case if he, or she in the case of a female religious, becomes a parent.

The conveyor belt out of ministry for priests or religious who become parents rests firmly upon this historic and deceivingly convincing argument.

Ministerial departure in every case, for the child's welfare, from their chosen profession is not aligned with support as standard, any help post-ministry is private and not guaranteed.

Cardinal Sean O'Malley in 2017, responding to the Boston Globe ground-breaking story on the children of priests and religious globally, commented, "if a priest fathers a child, he has a moral obligation to step aside from ministry and provide for the care and needs of the mother and the child. In such a moment, their welfare is the highest priority." (Cardinal Sean O'Malley, 2017)

His Eminences' statement stands out clear in my mind, but indeed many agree with him. Whilst the statement in and of itself seems laudable, "their welfare is the highest priority", what is lacking perhaps are practicalities. What would be better and indeed what would be an actualisation of what is right for a child would be the following, had His Eminence said the following, which unfortunately he did not.

"The priest/religious has a moral obligation to step aside from ministry and provide for the care and needs of the mother and the child. In such a moment, their welfare is the highest priority. Therefore, we are going to ensure that he or she in the case of female religious, will be given adequate housing, retraining where needed and if he or she was in a civil post, they would retain their professional position. All needs that are essential to the rearing of the child will be facilitated since it is the Catholic Church that wants the priest/religious to leave and not the other way around."

I do not believe that a priest/religious must always step aside from ministry to care for a child, as he can work in ministry and care for his child, openly so.

What is essential is not only *if* he takes care of his child, but *how* he takes care of his child?

If the ministerial departure was openly tailored with adequate supports in every case and this much was known and to be expected, like a redundancy package and a gold watch with warm wishes and cards saying, "you will be missed", that would be even -dare I say it- ok, for priests and religious to leave in every case. However, this is not the case.

Help post ministry is there, but private, not guaranteed and *ad hoc*.

Priests and religious are made to believe that they must choose one, bread and secrecy, or transparency and hunger. This is a form of emotional slavery. If the right thing was done, then I would not hear from girls in villages in parts of Africa, illiterate because their mothers could not educate them.

The situation is similar in India, not forsaking refugees left to their own devices in cities across Africa, whose fathers throw them out of the celebration of the eucharist, leaving them crying and baying for bread. There is a priest currently in Italy. I will not say where specifically. He got a woman pregnant and left the ministry. Now he is with his child, the mother and father did not marry, but he literally cannot afford bread. This is a hungry child in Italy, a father with no future and a home with no hope. Is this right?

Another priest in Colombia manages to feed his child. He remains in ministry. However, he cannot walk down the street with his child and be a parent. What he lacks is being able to emotionally support his child, since all concerned live in secrecy.

Several priests in Portugal also live lives of secrecy. They have contact with their children and the mothers, however, fear life outside ministry as no visible supports or assurances exist to assure them of support to transition to the lay state, financially, or in terms of housing and retraining not to mention the psychological loss of their priesthood.

Another priest in the United States, though he left the ministry, he remains there in his head. He finds it almost impossible to think in any way other, then as a priest. He has struggled to gain financial independence, and it has placed an unbearable strain upon his child and the child's mother. Many may blame him, however, in what other industry is a man penalised for being a parent?

Stories detailing illegal adoptions are common. One man told us about hearing from his father when he was a soldier during the war, that he was the son of a priest, thus commencing his internal battle, owing to the accompanying silence that came with the news. These stories of adoptive parents confessing to their adult children are as many as they are sad.

Whilst unusual circumstances, the absence of paperwork concerning the child, such as birth records, hospital visits and so forth, generate difficulties in such scenarios, it is the silence imposed that destroys.

If it is not the silence, the economic deprivation and poverty will certainly considerably lessen the quality of life for these children, as well as their mother and father.

What makes this incredibly sad is, there are some wonderful priests out there, marvellous men.

To this day, I work alongside the Catholic Church from the local level to the Vatican and have met incredible men, men who chose not to be fathers and that is a choice I respect.

Alongside the undeniable sadness that befalls the children, is a sadness that befalls these good men and indeed, women. Some of these people do their absolute best, daily, for people, their community, for decades, never putting a foot wrong, who work arduously yet, are unfairly associated with the horrendous crimes and neglect spoken of in this book. This is a crime in and of itself, and it is wrong and must be condemned.

To the men and women who have done no wrong, I ask you, do not do the wrong of continuing silence on this subject. Please break the code of non-acknowledgement and speak of what these pages talk of. It is only your voice that will give hope to the children, men and women hidden in the many pews of the worldwide Church in front of you, too terrified to move.

If you are reluctant to raise this issue, then you are most certainly part of the problem, this goes for laity equally.

In cases of silence surrounding a child of a priest, when and where a child is adopted, the mother of the child is often found to be a church worker, housekeeper, an accountant or another very creative post that allows the presence of the woman in question to remain, unquestioned. Many of these children have spoken to me and described their sadness at being abandoned

However, what separates these children who are adopted from other adopted children who are not fathered by Catholic clergy and religious is perhaps the extra layers of deception and obscurity surrounding the child and adoption, that would not normally accompany an adoption.

This phenomenon is not unique to children of Catholic priests. Children of Anglican clergy fathered out of wedlock have come to Coping advising of their paternity and the difficulties that ensued. I contacted the Archbishop of Canterbury regarding processes that surround children of Anglican clergy conceived out of wedlock. The Right Reverend Tim Thornton replied on the Archbishop's behalf in September 2020. I am grateful for his kindness.

This brief conversation might be viewed as confirmation children of clergy in other Christian Churches and Denominations also who suffer similar problems as children of Catholic Clergy/religious.

> **Doyle:** "If a child is conceived out of wedlock and the father is an Anglican priest, does the Anglican community condemn any attempt at silencing or veiling the paternity of the child to avoid/avert shame?"
>
> **The Right Reverend Tim Thornton:** "If this occurred in the Church of England then [...] the local Church of England authority or authorities would indeed condemn any attempt at silencing or veiling the paternity of the child."
>
> **Doyle:** "If an Anglican priest fathers a child and the relationship was out of wedlock, however, consensual, what is the professional fate of the priest in question? Will

he be allowed to remain in ministry, is it ad hoc/'case by case' or must he always leave ministry as a consequence?"

The Right Reverend Tim Thornton: "It is not possible to answer this question other than on a 'case by case' basis."

Doyle: "If in answer to question two, the priest is expected to resign or leave the ministry, will the Anglican community assist the former priest in gaining meaningful employment to support his child(ren)?"

The Right Reverend Tim Thornton: "Again given the answer to question 2 all that can be said is that of course support is offered to clergy who have to resign their office, but the circumstances would vary from case to case."

Doyle: "Does the Anglican community recognise that the intrinsic dignity of a child is recognised over and above any adult centred concerns surrounding possible embarrassment or shame and so forth and are responses centred on this child-centred belief or are norms in response to this phenomenon tailored with a preference for absolutist silence and cover-up?"

The Right Reverend Tim Thornton: "[...] Yes, the Church of England does recognise the intrinsic dignity and worth of every human and every child."

(The Right Reverend Tim Thornton Bishop at Lambeth., 2020.)

There is goodness in Reverend Thornton's words and the goodness achieved, regarding the children of the ordained to date, globally, is echoed and reaffirmed in his words, showing that many are on the same track so to speak.

It is heartening to see that "of course support is offered to clergy who have to resign their offices." However, support is not always on offer as is often the case for female religious globally who become pregnant.

"In November 1998, a four-page paper titled 'The Problem of the Sexual Abuse of African Religious in Africa and Rome' was presented by Missionaries of Our Lady of Africa Sr. Marie McDonald. [...] In McDonald's report, she states that 'sexual harassment and even rape of sisters by priests and bishops is allegedly common,' and that 'sometimes when a sister becomes pregnant, the priest insists that she have an abortion.'" (John L. Allen Jr., 2001)

Pope Francis acknowledged this issue, that is, sexual abuse of religious sisters. His Holiness' remarks were a response to a question posed by Associated Press journalist, Nicole Winfield.

"It is true, within the Church there have also been clerics who have done this; in some cultures, it is somewhat more prevalent than in others; [...], but there have been priests and even bishops who have done it. And I believe it may still be happening because it doesn't cease just by becoming aware of it [...] But it is a journey that goes further back [in time]. [...] There are cases, in some congregations, new ones in particular, and in some regions more than others." (Pope Francis., 2019)

Archbishop Eamon Martin mentioned, "the sexual assault and abuse of adults, including religious sisters" at the Vatican Sex Abuse Summit in 2019, as an issue which merits attention. (Archbishop Eamon Martin., 2019) The Archbishop was wise and correct to mention this issue, an issue the Pope himself recognises that "may still be happening."

> "On Feb. 18, 1995, Cardinal Eduardo Martínez, prefect of the Vatican congregation for religious life, along with members of his staff, were briefed on the problem by Medical Missionary of Mary Sr. Maura O'Donohue, a physician. O'Donohue is responsible for a 1994 report that constitutes one of the more comprehensive accounts."
>
> (John L. Allen Jr., 2001)

Sister O'Donohue notes,

> "in several countries, sisters are troubled by policies that require them to leave the congregation if they become pregnant, while the priest involved is able to continue his ministry. Beyond fairness is the question of social justice, since the sister is left to raise the child as a single parent, 'often with a great deal of stigmatization and frequently in very poor socioeconomic circumstances. I was given examples in several countries where such women were forced into becoming a second or third wife in a family because of lost status in the local culture. The alternative,

as a matter of survival, is to go 'on the streets' as prostitutes' and thereby 'expose themselves to the risk of HIV, if not already infected.'" (John L. Allen Jr., 2001) Twenty plus years on, treatment of female religious remains an issue. Vatican Prefect and Cardinal Braz de Aviz notes, referencing female religious who leave the ministry, "sometimes they are completely abandoned." (Cardinal João Braz de Aviz, 2020) Cardinal De Aviz further notes in relation to renewal within religious life.

"In many cases, the relationship between consecrated men and women represents a sick system of relations of submission and dominance that takes away the sense of freedom and joy, a misunderstood obedience." (Allen, 2020)

In February 2020, Cardinal De Aviz answered questions concerning female religious who leave ministry and support for said former religious.

"[...] There have also been a few cases of prostitution in order to support themselves. These are ex-sisters! [...] We must change the attitude of rejection, the temptation to ignore these people, to say 'it is no longer our problem.' And then, often these ex-sisters are not accompanied in any way, not a word is said to help them... all this must absolutely change.'"

(Cardinal João Braz de Aviz, 2020)

Whilst the desire to change the attitude that suggests, "'it is no longer our problem", requires change and the Vatican agree, this was made known over two decades ago and only now are the words, "all this must absolutely change", being said.

"Completely abandoned", "not accompanied", "a sick system of relations." These words convey the living reality for female religious and former female religious, and consequently, this is the domestic setting for their offspring. There must be a change.

However, change begins with the recognition of the fact that it took more than two decades for the Vatican to say, "all this must absolutely change."

These words are welcomed, but behind the intention is a system of rejection that is ingrained in the clerical world, a rejection that impinges upon children of the ordained and religious, this systemic disposition must be unearthed.

I reached out to Sister McDonald.

Sister Maura O'Donohue has died although her legacy surrounding the treatment of her religious sisters remains.

I asked Sister McDonald a question, early in the summer of 2020. Her devotion to those who suffer in this regard truly is impressive.

> "Regarding your sisters in Christ, for those (Cann. 702 §2), what is your hope for them as you look forward?"

Sister McDonald states.

> "My hope for them is that free from all that might hold them prisoner...they will be able to fulfil God's dream for them and live their lives and their vocation to the full bringing joy and hope to many." (Sister Marie McDonald, 2020.)

Sister McDonald echoes the sentiment of her reports, wherein she highlighted the maltreatment of religious sisters of whom some who become pregnant and are subsequently "punished by dismissal from the congregation." (John L. Allen Jr., 2001)

But her admirable desire to see her religious sisters, and undoubtedly their children, "free from all that might hold them prisoner" remains.

Sexual abuse in Africa, juxtaposed alongside mothers dismissed owing to pregnancy, children fathered by Anglican clergy outside of wedlock, priests who leave ministry adhering to the notion that it is the moral thing to do, former religious sisters forced into prostitution, what I dub, 'the Moral Argument' is an unethical shroud disguised linguistically as an ethical act which harms.

However, it hastens all priests and religious who have become parents through a narrow gap, many of whom suffer unemployment (men and women alike), hunger and deprivation. This is not Catholic.

> "No sacrifice made by adults will be considered too costly or too great, if it means the child never has to feel that he or she is a mistake, or worthless or abandoned to the four winds and the arrogance of man" (Pope Francis, 2016),

Then why are these children and their parents suffering?

Why not establish a more reliable norm for these children, than one of regret which nurtures *Silentium* in a prenatal, somatic fashion propagating child neglect? They are suffering because the language of the Moral Argument, whilst ethically enticing is simultaneously impractical, especially for former religious in developing countries.

Post-ministerial difficulties for new parents (former religious) was noted by Professor Emeritus Fr. D. Vincent Twomey SVD who confirms, the following regarding priest and religious finding suitable employment post-ministry.

> "Every effort should be made by Church authorities to help them find suitable employment, which may not be easy for a priest (or indeed, at times, for a female religious) who has no other professional qualifications." (Twomey, 2020) Professor Twomey further commented, "sisters who leave the religious life are mostly trained as nurses, teachers, cooks, etc., and are generally playable in their profession, but others, such as contemplative nuns would have no such training." (Twomey., 2020)

Fr D Vincent Twomey SVD is a former doctoral student of Pope Benedict XVI. Eloquently, he highlighted the difficulties and underpinned by Sister O'Donohue and Sister McDonald. Whilst the Vatican in 2020 recognises "relations of submission and dominance that takes away the sense of freedom and joy", noting "a misunderstood obedience", little has been done pragmatically speaking.

The freedom desired by Sister McDonald, who bravely highlighted the plight of female religious alongside Sister O'Donohue, so they might bring "joy and hope", is replaced with a default condition of being "punished by dismissal from the congregation" and the trauma she and her child endure thereafter is unimaginable.

Returning to Rome, in the context of female religious, a body, a union of female religious exists called the UISG.

The mission of the UISG (Union of International Superiors General) is as follows.

> "The mission of UISG is to build bridges that span distances, borders and boundaries in order to create ways for members to be in communication, in community and in communion. The purpose of UISG is to promote an understanding of religious life." (UISG, 2020)

Coping raised this issue with the UISG, the Union of Female Superior's General, noting two questions:

1. If a religious sister becomes pregnant, whether consensually or criminally, if she decides to leave the Order, what (if any) practical supports, in terms of employment assistance, retraining and housing are available to her and her child post-departure?

2. If a Religious Sister gives the child up for adoption having become pregnant, may she remain an active member of the Order afterwards? Cardinal Stella made a statement recently, which indicated a religious might stay in religious life having become a parent if the child enters a "consolidated family." Is it the same for religious women who prefer adoption for their child, or is it different for religious sisters? Must religious women leave active ministry always - whilst men can remain - as indicated by His Eminence, however "rare" these exceptions may be or, may women also have the chance to stay. Is this door closed or open?

The UISG issued their reply in September 2019.

"While there is no special reference in canon law to the case of a sister who becomes pregnant, canon 702 §2 requires each institute 'to observe equity and charity of the gospel towards a member who is separated from it.' Each institute has, therefore, its own policies regarding the provision of financial and other types of support which take both the context and the personal circumstance into account, when a member leaves a religious congregation. These provisions would most certainly apply in the case of a sister becoming pregnant [...]. If the pregnancy arose without consent on part of the sister, either through rape or abuse of power, there would be a special duty of care on the part of all concerned, to ensure the well-being of both the child and the mother. [The letter also states that the UISG] is also aware of a small number of cases where the sister left her congregation during pregnancy, gave birth to her child and then gave the child up for adoption before [she] returned to the convent. In some of these cases, the sister later re-established contact with her child." (UISG, 2019)

This charitably sidesteps the horrendous destitution suffered by female religious who are mothers. If religious orders are called to "observe equity and charity of the gospel towards a member who is separated from it", yet nuns have worked as prostitutes and entered questionable marriages, then, the church has acted improperly, ethically, morally and canonically.

'Very poor socioeconomic circumstances' were highlighted by Sister O'Donohue in Allen and Schaeffer's 2001 article where 'the sister is left to raise the child as a single parent', 'often with a great deal of stigmatization' she notes. 'I was given examples in several countries where such women were forced into becoming a second or third wife in a family because of lost status in the local culture.' Sister O'Donohue notes.

> "Superior generals I have met were extremely concerned about the harassment sisters were experiencing from priests in some areas. One superior of a diocesan congregation, where several sisters became pregnant by priests, has been at a complete loss to find an appropriate

solution. Another diocesan congregation has had to dismiss over 20 sisters because of pregnancy, again in many cases by priests. [Sister O'Donohue further notes] [some] have actually encouraged abortion for sisters with whom they have been involved. Some Catholic medical professionals employed in Catholic hospitals have reported pressure being exerted on them by priests to procure abortions in those hospitals for religious sisters."

(John L. Allen Jr., 2001)

Sister O'Donoghue further notes.

"In another country, a recent convert from Islam (one of two daughters who became Christians) was accepted as a candidate to a local religious congregation. When she went to her parish priest for the required certificates, she was subjected to rape by the priest before being given the certificates. Having been disowned by her family because of becoming a Christian, she did not feel free to return home. She joined the congregation and soon afterwards found she was pregnant. To her mind, the only option for her was to leave the congregation, without giving the reason. She spent 10 days roaming the forest, agonizing over what to do. Then she decided to go and talk to the bishop, who called in the priest. The priest accepted the accusation as true and was told by the bishop to go on a two-week retreat." (John L. Allen Jr., 2001)

"All this must absolutely change" notes Cardinal De Aviz. Cardinal De Aviz' statement concerning the abuse of religious is welcomed. Still, it needs to be actualised in terms of a solution.

Vincent Twomey, alongside Sister O'Donohue and Sister McDonald, correctly highlight the plight of former religious who suffer. However, what do we do to stop it as opposed to only condemning it with no further action?

One needs to be careful of not falling into the trap of continually blaming, condemning and not fixing a troubling situation.

It appears that is what has happened here, affecting women and children grievously. Is there a central problem, an axis upon which most post-ministerial issues come from? Yes, there is!

Imagine this. A company adopt a policy that any employee who becomes a parent must leave their job. Whether you are a man or a woman, you are gone. You are gone under the banner of "lamentable defection" (Pope Saint Paul VI., 1967.) You have caused "scandal" (cann. 277 §2). This scandal socially baptises the child conceived with shame, isolation, and stigma. The mother and father may endure poverty and deprivation and all because of one's responsibility as a parent to provide for a child.

What would be the first response of the Catholic Church toward this newly adopted policy? Catholicism socially drips with promoted equality; the papacy of His Holiness Pope Francis has been one characterised by going out to the margins.

> "Indeed, the life that we are called to promote and defend is not an abstract concept, but rather it is always manifested in a person in flesh and blood: a baby who has just been conceived, a marginalized poor person, a sick person who is disheartened or in a terminal ill state, one who has lost their job or cannot find one, a rejected or

marginalized migrant.... Life manifests itself tangibly in people." (Pope Francis., 2020)

Then, if the needs of raped, prostituted former female religious remain, if former religious "forced into becoming a second or third wife in a family because of lost status in the local culture" still endure this pain, indeed if it is "still happening", as hinted at by His Holiness, Catholicism must go to these margins. The needs of mothers, fathers, and the children of the ordained and religious, however, still exist. Truly then, the children of priests, religious and their mothers and fathers, living in a vacuum suffocating from non-acknowledgement, deserve better than "tut, tut, that's awful" with the song of crickets taking the place of pragmatic action.

The loss of dignity of priest-fathers who suffer unemployment might be juxtaposed alongside the loss of dignity, as suffered by female religious. I am speaking about men who have not raped, men who fathered children consensually, not by force or via power imbalance, and as a result must join the children of priests and religious and their mothers outside and beyond the margins.

There at the border of what is socially acceptable to treat, those who are on the margins of society receive adequate care, and that is good. But outside and beyond, those who treat the marginalised, turn a blind eye to their own neglected and secret offspring, to their brother priests and religious sisters, whose hand is now dry in the arid sun from want of charity and assistance.

The central problem, the common problem that former priests and religious suffer and consequently, their children is, continence is promoted openly and collectively. In contrast, charity toward the children of the ordained and religious and their parents is supported privately.

On an individualised basis, charity toward these marginalised persons is not promoted as widely as chastity is. Continence means abstaining from all sexual activity. Continence is not the problem. It is a question of priorities and prioritising children, charity and equity. Thus, the law of celibacy, which means unmarried, reliably juxtaposed with chastity, is put forth primarily, openly, ahead of the need to provide for those who defect. It should be the other way around. Behind and beneath that law, like ants squirming beneath a block scrambling for food, hiding when a ray of light appears, for fear they might be exposed, are children, mothers and fathers, socially excluded.

If you cannot as a priestly and religious body be collectively celibate and chaste, this inability does not give rise to an automatic right to respond to that human inability, fostering situations where children and their parents suffer. It is in the separation of the parents of children of the ordained from celibate and chaste priests and religious that preserves exclusivity surrounding chaste celibacy, a character of being absolute. The exclusion and removal of said persons remove those who personify "scandal" (cann. 277 §2) from those who are perceived as being chaste and celibate.

The intention of the act of removal from the ministry is disguised as being in the best interests of the child. If the practice of doing what was right for the child was real, such an action would be characterised by the open provision of housing, retraining, employment. But it is not. Whilst some orders and dioceses may provide privately, this sustenance is neither guaranteed nor foreseeable, and it is this uncertainty that promotes silence, *Silentium.*

Offsetting suspicion regarding the suspected predominance of children of the ordained is equally an issue. Statements such as,

> "the instance of when a priest has fathered a child has not been very frequent" (Cardinal Sean O'Malley, 2017) are unhelpful.

> Such sentiments feed the narrative of belief many that children of priests and religious buy into, which proclaims, "I'm the only one!"

With every respect owing, in my experience, it is the Bishop and the Diocese/Archdiocese/Religious Order, which is the very last to know of such situations, given the circumstances.

To quote Sister McDonald, "only if we can look at it honestly will we be able to find solutions" (John L. Allen Jr., 2001).

This means avoiding generalisations that deflect attention away from an issue or paint it as seemingly not a cause for alarm. This is a real worry for Coping. Therefore, Coping pushed for the release of the Vatican Guidelines for the children of the ordained. The Vatican Guidelines for the children of the ordained contain two exceptions allowing priests/religious to remain in ministry, guideline three and four outlines the exceptions. The following is taken from the Vatican Guidelines section of Coping International's website including the addendum that follows.

> III. "The presence of children [...] was treated, de facto, as a practically automatic reason [...] [for] dispensation. [...] The loss of the clerical state is imposed because paternal responsibility creates permanent obligations that in the legislation of the Latin Church does not provide for the exercise of priestly ministry." However, "exceptions" include "the case of a new-born, the child of a priest, who in a particular situation enters into a family already consolidated, in which another parent assumes [...] the role of the father." (Stella.)

IV. "In the situation where a priest who has "children who are already grown up, 20- 30 years old [...], in these situations, the Dicastery does not oblige the Bishop to invite the priests to request the dispensation" from priesthood owing to paternity. "The Dicastery counsels a more flexible discernment within the rigorous practise and guidelines of the Congregation." (Stella.)

"Addendum to Guidelines:

The Vatican clarified the third guideline relating to 'consolidated families' confirming that any such priest who remains in ministry who is the father of a new-born, the timing and the manner of conveying information relating to his paternity rests with the interested adults (biological parents/guardians). Regarding the situation whereupon a priest fathers' a child but neither biological parent wish to marry, regarding the impossibility of a priest remaining in the priesthood, recommitting to celibacy and acknowledging his child (openly), the Holy See agreed that such a situation is not impossible, but that each case is examined on its own merits and its own particular circumstances, adding that many considerations must be taken into account, including the suitability of the priest for the priesthood. If a priest has fathered a child, one must consider two things: 1) the good of the child, all we have to do for that, keeping in mind any concrete situation, 2) the suitability of the priest for the priesthood and for exercising ministry. The Holy See agreed that secrecy is not required in situations where children of priests exist but proper discernment as to when to tell the child (ensuring emotional stability of the child to receive said news so they are supported) beautifully citing the Gospel according to John 16:12, Coping fully concurs with this position. The Holy See has further commented upon the use of confidentiality agreements also noting the primacy of the good of the child, as per Irish Bishops 2015." (Coping International., 2020)

Now the challenge is actualising these guidelines.

If a priest wishes to remain in ministry and provide for his child, then he can. Whilst a female religious may want to leave, her departure should not mean a release from any civil post she may have, teaching, nursing and so forth. She should be allowed to remain in this post. If she possesses no such professional qualification, she should be assisted in terms of housing, retraining and sufficient sustenance to get her to a position where she may care for her child.

Morality must always be structured with pragmatism. That is, how will one actualise that which you call the parent to do? If you call them to carry out an act, because it is the moral thing to do but do not equip them with the skills or tools to carry out the said act, then you knowingly contribute to the non-completion of the moral action, in this case, to care for a child. Put simply, you contribute to a child being hungry, uncertain, afraid, or fearful.

The system of the automatic expulsion of priests and religious (who become parents) lies at the very heart of *Silentium* and is linked with the mental health issues, themselves connected with non-acknowledgement.

The brokenness lies not in the system of celibacy and promoted chastity, but in the inadequate response of the Catholic Church when chastity and celibacy are absent, forsaken. Breaking clerical chastity risks inflicting brokenness upon a child, unemployment and so forth. This brokenness is disguised as a moral and ethical act, veiled beneath moralistic language. In this, stepping aside becomes synonymous with providing critical care for a child.

Conscious of this problem of the deceptiveness of the Moral Argument, I turned to the Irish Bishops once again. The Bishops of Ireland have been instrumental in creating and validating a global solution to a problem never openly addressed in history before. Their presence and contribution can in no way be undervalued, underestimated, or understated, and I can only thank them, I pray God will reward them.

> "It is not possible to rule out, at the beginning, any possible response to these situations [relating the situation where a priest fathers a child] which involves a simple default position of insisting that a man 'leave the priesthood' or that he automatically be permitted to continue in active

ministry. All reasonable and fair options should be considered as possible, so this neither rules in or rules out various outcomes." (Irish Catholic Bishops Conference., 2018)

This, thankfully, sent out ripples across the world. The French Bishops wrote to Coping having been initially contacted by Coping. They adopted a similar position to Cardinal Stella and the Irish Bishops, noting the *ad hoc* nature of this situation.

They note in their April 2019 letter to Coping, and the following is translated from the original in French, which is available on Coping, under 'episcopacy' as are the subsequent episcopal statements including original languages, they were first stated in.

> "The French episcopate looks first when a cleric becomes the father of a child, the good of the latter and the need for him to be able to benefit from an education where his father is present. This is why he asks the father to take his responsibilities by renouncing the clerical state. It could be otherwise when the paternity of a cleric is discovered when his child has already acquired an autonomy according to his age. [This ties in neatly with Cardinal Stella's cited

exceptions/Vatican guidelines.]" (French Episcopal Conference., 2019)

The Maltese Episcopacy wrote to Coping.

"The bishops committed themselves to receive and accompany anyone who approaches them on this issue. Those concerned can make contact with them [...] [further noting] your correspondence was forwarded to the Safeguarding Commission of the Archdiocese of Malta so that it will be taken into consideration when revising our policies in this area." (Maltese Episcopal Conference, 2018)

The Bishops of England and Wales similarly responded to Coping in July 2018.

"With regard to Children of the Ordained and religious, every bishop in England and Wales would want to discern the best ways in which it is possible for the father of a child, who is a priest, to fulfil his responsibilities. Every bishop in England and Wales is willing to meet anyone in their diocese in a similar situation. With regard to a priest who has become a father, the Bishops of England and Wales recognise that it is not possible to rule out, at the beginning, any possible responses to these situations, which involve a simple default position of insisting that a man 'leave the priesthood' or that he automatically be permitted to continue in active ministry." (Catholic Bishops Conference of England & Wales., 2018)

The Bishops of Scotland similarly responded.

"It is the policy of the Bishops of Scotland that they will meet with and listen to those who approach them on a case by case basis and consider their requests. To answer your specific question as to whether counselling will be provided, each Bishop will look into such requests on a case by case basis, and with the help of professional advice." (Catholic Bishops Conference of Scotland Episcopal Secretary., 2014)

In a further statement, the Scottish Bishops made in 2018 regarding children of priests, the Bishops stated,

"with regard to a priest who has become a father, the Bishops recognise that it is not possible to rule out, at the beginning, any possible responses to these situations, which involve a simple default position of insisting that a man "leave the priesthood" or that he automatically be permitted to continue in active ministry. Each case should be judged on its merits." (Catholic Bishops Conference of Scotland., 2018)

Then the Portuguese weighed in on the issue on whether a priest must leave the priesthood having fathered a child. The Portuguese Bishops Conference became aware of the issue of children of priests following revelations of cases in Portugal and intervention from Coping.

"Questioned on the issue of priests who have children and their possible treatment in Portugal, [Cardinal] Manuel Clemente, [Cardinal-Patriarch of Lisbon] said that the CEP follows the position of the Holy See: 'If someone has a child, he is responsible for that child.'" (Cardinal Manuel Clemente, 2019)

At that same press conference, João Francisco Gomes, a journalist for *Observador* newspaper in Portugal, asked a question of Cardinal Clemente. Gomes had become interested in the issue of children of priests after completing an interview with me in Rome in 2019. Following the interview, Mr Gomes remained in contact with me on a professional basis, relating to matters about Portugal and Coping. Gomes emailed me after the Portuguese Bishops press conference stating,

> "I asked cardinal Clemente about this subject [of whether [a] priest must always leave the priesthood having fathered a child.] He stated clearly that dismissal from the clerical state must be considered 'case by case.'" (Gomes, 2019)

The importance of pushing case by case is that case by case eliminates, 'in every case' which erodes the default position, which promotes choice, albeit indirectly.

What Sister O'Donohue and Sister McDonald highlighted, what Cardinal De Aviz condemned (mistreatment of female religious) and indeed what Sister O'Donohue still prays for "[freedom] from all that might hold them prisoner" can be attained. They can be achieved if we put the human first, not traditions.

The Moral Argument stops short of acknowledging these fears outlined in this chapter. The Moral Argument must be dissected, eroded and, in its place, a new model of treating and remedying what is referred to as the "wound" of lamentable defection or procreative "lamentable defection" by Pope Saint Paul VI, in 1967. This ancient argument ignores individual needs and ignores absent employment perspective, retraining and housing needs to fulfil said moral obligation. It exists as a bandage of morality, an audible and pastorally acceptable bandage which uses words such as "...go and care for your child", however, provides little hint of how to provide said care. In other words, the Moral Argument begets domestic destitution which fosters child neglect.

If we continue to demand that all priests and religious leave ministry without a clue as to how they can provide for their child outside the ministry, what we are doing is audibly promoting care for the child, but not pragmatically. We are sending women and men into a social wilderness without a care as to how they may provide for the forthcoming child. That is not Catholic.

You cannot send any employee, whether they are a road sweeper or a bishop into inevitable unemployment, possible homelessness and all that goes with that, owing to paternity, you just can't, it is a matter of social justice. You cannot adopt a policy of inevitable expulsion and disguise it as being child-centred. Yet, that corporate strategy exists and in part fosters unemployment, hunger, impoverished situations for mothers and neglect of children and denotes this policy Catholic.

This is the reason the Vatican began to recognise this as an issue and released the guidelines for children of priests in 2020, which included exceptions allowing priests/religious to remain in ministry having become a parent. How can Catholicism stand, if within the glaring light of the *Son*, shadowed, lay marginalised children by scorned and abused women; hidden, behind forgotten fathers, who seek bread, so their own might not go hungry?

Indeed, their cry for housing, employment and food is drowned out by meaningless moralistic sentiment, prayer without bread, as back beneath imposed shadows they crawl, where they have been for centuries. This is not about condemning but challenging and promoting growth. If Catholicism cannot reach out realistically, minus unrealistic sentiment, to the children of the ordained and religious supporting their parents, openly, then what is Catholicism, or indeed, what has it become, when stood against with its Christocentric origins?

The Bible says,

> "the child will not share the guilt of the parent" (Ezekiel 18:20)

Though the child may not share the guilt, if children of the ordained are not prioritised, they indeed share in consequence of the guilt of clerical infidelity, via the Moral Argument.

Why punish the children of the ordained via the Moral Argument with a father or mother expelled from ministry owing to the child's existence, where neither mother nor father is certain of their future? To do this is to punish children intergenerationally. To do this is anti-Catholic, as the conscience understands foreseeable indirect action and liability from a moral perspective, poverty is a foreseeable indirect consequence of unemployment.

> "Fighting against abuse means fostering and empowering communities capable of watching over and announcing that all life deserves to be respected and valued, especially that of the most defenceless who do not have the resources to make their voices heard." (Pope Francis., 2020)

Can the community of the Catholic church initiate change so as to care for their own children or, will they choose to continue to pretend all is well, knowingly enabling emotional harm of the children of the ordained via the Moral Argument? The culture of psychological and emotional abuse will continue relentlessly via what Pope Saint Paul VI called the "lamentable defection", itself procreative. Thus, the procreative "lamentable defection", is responded to appropriately with something other than the Moral Argument. If the children of the ordained and their parents are not responded to responsibly, then, unfortunately, the culture of abuse will continue in an unstoppable manner.

To the seminarian, as you gaze into a future of sacrifice walking as Simon with the Christ, in His sacrifice, know that if you drop that cross of chastity and celibacy that you so willingly take up, it could fall upon the mind of a child in the womb, your child, creating a ripple of destruction that the church is grappling to deal with. Are you capable of upholding this sacrifice?

> "If one is called to be Catholic, one follows what the Church teaches; that is the correct understanding of conscience (as upheld also by Vatican II). And if one really cannot follow

what the Church teaches, then one's conscience requires that one leave the Church. That is the adult decision. One's conscience does not require that one makes up one's own personal religion and then pretend that it is Catholic." (Bishop Robert C. Morlino., 2012)

So, one respects children. I could not have put it better myself!

Chapter Four.

Parēns.

JJ was dead just eight years when I first arrived at the doors of Maynooth College in Kildare, Ireland.

My beloved Godfather, whom I kept nestled in my the back of my heart, had -without my knowing- influenced me to the point that I departed Dublin, having studied languages, bound for Maynooth, County Kildare, to study theology not fully knowing why?

If you are unfamiliar with what the word Maynooth means in the Irish social consciousness, it conjures another word, "priests."

The word 'Maynooth' of course does not mean 'priests', Maynooth is the name of a small town, outside of Dublin, in County Kildare, in the East of Ireland. Maynooth is synonymous with priesthood since it is the home of the National Irish Seminary, Saint Patrick's College.

It is also my *Alma Mater* and a place of respite for me to this day. The grounds are extensive, painted with wildlife and beautifully arranged trees which shadow impressively large greenery.

It is a place of reflection, where the chorus of nature, sing to amateur and seasoned theologians alike.

I started studying at Maynooth in 2003 and graduated four years later with a bachelor's degree in Theology and English.

However, Maynooth was never about attaining a piece of paper for me. Maynooth was and remains to be, a reconnection with some interior part of me, a role I could not fathom? I entered Maynooth in 2003 and graduated in 2007, and I first found out that I was Fr. JJ's son in 2011. So, before my understanding, some part of me felt interiorly connected with the priesthood, yet I was unsure why?

I at times tried explaining this, the innate compulsion I felt toward Catholicism and elements of Catholicism.

One of my mentors, one evening in his study, said to me, "it is called *votum Ecclesiae*." He defined it as a desire for church, the "implicit and unconscious desire (*implicitum votum Ecclesiae*) to enter the Catholic fold." (Harrison)

For me, the *votum Ecclesiae* was interwoven, as a spiritual phenomenon with a human phenomenon, psychology. That is, my encounter with God remembered encounters with my father, the Catholic priest, that also, were internal and in the realm of the unspoken. However, being among priests made sense to me. I had no idea why? Of course, what I was connecting was myself or rather, whom I was connecting with was myself. I was integrating, my inner child, who literally spent the entirety of my childhood with a priest, felt secure among "priest", "church", and so forth.

I did not associate this feeling of being at home and atonement with my inner child seeking out peace and that peace I had with my late (at the time, unknown father) then. Instead, I interpreted it as a desire for church, which owing to my family, many of whom entered the priesthood and religious life, would of course not be far from the truth. In other words, the apple didn't fall far from the proverbial tree. The apple dropped firmly in Maynooth.

This desire for Church in me came to a point at an unusual time when the Catholic Church was immersed in the child sex abuse scandal.

Society was increasingly becoming secularised, and religion had considerably less influence over people and culture than it once had. Conversely, I seemingly, was going in the opposite direction? Something internally, instinctually drew me to the church in a society that was at the time, anti-church.

I was horrified at disclosures that emanated regarding clerical crimes. Nonetheless, I felt drawn to Maynooth and toward the church and still do today, in the capacity as someone who wants to bring some healing.

This world brought me interior comfort. There was an innate sense of peace I felt while studying, somehow when I was around Catholicism and priesthood, I felt at home, as I did in the presbytery with my father as a child, watching MacGyver after dinner, though unbelievably I never connected the two.

My father started studying at a seminary in 1959.

Forty-four years later, his son stepped into Maynooth, oblivious to his clerical paternity.

Indeed, in my case, the apple did not fall far from the tree.

Curiously, this feeling of being at home while in Maynooth nurtured the whole idea of being called to be atoned and close to God.

The degree to which God called me and the degree to which I called upon God looking for my father, albeit unconsciously, is something that a lifetime of discernment might determine?

However, I was at home at Maynooth. To this day, I go on short breaks, retreats to my *Alma Mater*, thinking, breathing, soaking in the historicity, the hope contained therein witnessed in the youthfulness of a new Church budding in undergraduate Theologians, as they scribble on endless reams of cheap paper.

I was always conscious that the next Augustine or Aquinas, Bishop, Pope or Saint, may childishly be slumbered in our midst, maybe next to me.

It was within these hallowed halls of Maynooth Seminary that I a lay student was formed theologically speaking. During those formative years, mornings were spent attending classes. Moral Theology particularly interested me. The term elevenses was first introduced to me in Maynooth, when mid-morning, lessons and life stopped for twenty minutes, a coffee break in Pugin hall. Discernment and reflection played a role in the formative academic process of Maynooth. This is the best part of the place. This discerning atmosphere tastes of coffee, ardent like the intent on the faces of the new energetic theologians who now can explain curious mysteries of the Catholic Church, or so they believed.

The halls and walls of this place for me brought me home into a place where I had not been for almost a decade, and I had no idea why. My unconscious had steered me here, I feel.

The many halls of Maynooth seminary are framed with black and white photos of men ordained to the priesthood, dating back to the twentieth century.

Upstairs, the images date back to the beginning of the twentieth century. The ornate calligraphy evoked respect. I examined the faces of these men, now dead and wondered at the expectation in their faces at that moment the photo was taken, anticipation, eagerness, now at the mercy of God, for they are long since deceased, may they rest in peace. History at Maynooth fell like dust from the walls and statues, illuminated by the light of tutorage, hope and ink.

Months and years were spent in wide-open classrooms, with men and women of all ages, our lecturer sitting at the top of the class, but on a desk, feet on a chair.

Fr. Hugh Connolly was on our level. He engaged with us. Questions surrounding bioethics, euthanasia, the just war theory, the ethics of related matters that affected every person seated were discussed and finished with, "yes, *but!*"

The hour would go in just a minute. It was never a chore and always a blessing. However, what these years did, was engage a curious mind, a wandering, wondering mind.

I felt as if my mind was an orphan, dropped off deep within the institution of the Catholic Church. I began to think, wander, and take it all in, questioning and believing at the same time. Yet, I was at home strangely, firmly, and perhaps more so than my classmates were?

I recognised something within the priests and seminarians. There was something deeply familiar about them. I thought it to be holiness itself, but it seemed to be more personal than that? Why did I feel at home here?

What I would learn in time, was that what I was recognising was not so much priesthood, more a certain priest, wrapped up within the context of the priesthood, that I unconsciously realised. They raised the priest in my mind, yet secrecy blurred his face from me. The presence of religiosity wrought all the sentiments and feelings that I felt in the presence of JJ as a child, in echoing Churches in a seemingly endless sea of the clergy.

Like the child, familiar with the sweetened smell of the carpenter's wood, inhaling childhood at their father's feet, picking up the wood shavings from the dusty floor as the autumn sunshine glittered upon the carpenter's tools, I too recognised my father, amid a blackened sea of hope.

In the distance, I saw a white beacon of truth amid their presence, yet it was close enough to remind me, taking me back, again and again, reminding me of something good and wholesome.

These feelings rising like yeast, in the embers of my soul, were something that I had long forgotten, yet the inner child told this distracted scholar of goodness once known, once shown, before he, my priest, was hidden by death and secrecy. Deep within priesthood was my father, and I was on a journey, a mysterious journey that would end and begin with a poem, a simple poem, the written word.

The years at Maynooth were as if I had a dream, and suddenly it was over. The overall sense of belonging was flanked by surprise and grief, akin to another mysterious grief that welled up in me when I was just a boy. It was not that it was a secret, looking back, it's that they didn't say it.

I was in JJ's car when it happened, when he died, my best pal, my friend, my confidant, my king. I slowly walked back toward the house, leaving behind the Punto he had bought just months before. It was a bright June afternoon. The full blossom of nature betrayed the end that crept within me like a demon, inside a child. I did not want this. I approached the hall. Those present in the house when his soul rose to God, as my stomach sank, parted, like an automatic guard of honour and I none the wiser. There was nothing honourable about it. Instead of comforting, I was stared at and nodded at surreptitiously. They all knew, I didn't, not fully at least.

I turned the corner and could see the door, one person in the room and a corpse lying warmly on a bed. He was gone. He had left me, this priest, this wonderful priest, this man I loved so much.

"Vin, your dad is dead." These are the words that were whispered to me as I was ushered toward a corpse. His familiar hair gently caressed his warm forehead as his weary body, deep within a white vest, had given up. The sheets warmth betrayed the cool hand of death that had just swept through them, and there was nothing that I could do about it.

He was gone.

Those important words, those so crucial words, "your dad is dead" quickly slipped out of my ear not to be remembered for almost twenty years.

It was all just too much to bear, I guess. However, I could not grieve, for he was father to everyone else, but me.

I slept in a chair that night by his bed, only to wake at 4 am vomiting with fright. The trembling grief inside of me reasoned with JJ's now rubbery complexion, urging him to move, if only a little bit. I watched his eyelid, my heart thrashing within me, awaiting a single movement, yet as my eyes dried from not blinking, I slowly but regretfully recognised the death that by now, had grown so cold within me, I could not even cry. I retired to bed and didn't wake for what seemed like many heavy years.

They buried him mid-week. He died on a Pentecost Sunday. "He would have liked that," someone remarked. I didn't like it, but that didn't seem to matter to many.

His grave was dug by the neighbours, lined with wildflowers.

The nurses, carers and some family, robed like a king. It was weird seeing him dressed up in all his regalia. I had no idea that JJ had robes and was so important?

Patiently and correctly, with nods of agreement on faces that did not shed a tear, the coffin's lowering straps slipped and burned the calloused, sallow hands of the gravediggers, marked with clay and years.

Nobody said a word as they took him from me, lowering him slowly but surely away from me, not acknowledging my rising fear.

They laid him among the blossoms that would soon die, in his fading memory, in the cold black earth, beneath a blue night in June.

I could not talk of my dead king, it is not as if he was my father, or so I believed.

I buried the fullness of my grief in a small letter with him. I told him how much I missed him, I told him only stuff we knew, and as I write these words, it is the first time I have remembered the existence of this little letter, since my twelve-year-old hand released that small note beneath his purple robes, to lie by his priestly heart forever. The roots of my anguish lay in blue, mottled ink on a torn page. Its origins are as torn as my own yet buried with care. That, it seems, is the only care that the children of the ordained may count on; that their identity and the fullness of that identity is buried with care, so as to assure the adults concerned, society and church that the child will not pose a threat anymore or ever, that is the care we can rely on, that much is almost guaranteed.

The cold, dry clay buried in the hands of the gravediggers shook like holy water to the ground in the glaring sunlight. Then, the finality of the barren echo of clods of earth that escaped the priest's hands fell like hard rain upon the coffin, echoing in the dead, still, silence heaving around the grave wherein he lay, motionless as my tiny, joined hands, and I unable to pray a single word.

Occasional words from the Our Father or the Hail Mary, words JJ had taught me, slid out of my mouth in place of tears as I stood by his grave. A tarpaulin was then pulled over the open grave, and the open wound in my heart, both were thought to be buried indefinitely. I peeked one last time beneath the false covering at the coffin now alone in the earth, a final glimpse at this priest that meant so much to me, not understanding fully, why I loved him so much?

I spent years ambling the framed halls of Maynooth, curious, academically, and personally. I chatted numerous seminarians and whilst the friendship was genuine, I could never figure out why this place and these conversations calmed me, and it would only be looking back reflectively, on May 19th 2011, when I found out about my dad, that this entire process would make sense, a process inspired by God, I feel and all for a purpose maybe?

What was happening, behind the scenes, was the son of a man, who had similar interests, was dropped off at virtually the same door many years.

As the years passed, I came to know the people that I studied with, young men and women who had a love of academia and almost all of whom, were spiritually inclined as I was.

Among them, a young seminarian named Yousef Yakoub, from Israel.

Yousef was training to be a priest within the Maronite Catholic tradition which enjoys full communion with the Pope and Rome. What separated Yousef from other seminarians and what curiously intrigued me was the fact that in December 2009, when he was ordained a Catholic priest, his wife was present. His brother priests who were ordained with him that day were to become celibate priests, Yousef returned home a married Catholic priest.

Within the Catholic Church, there are many different rites of the priesthood, all of which share the same theological vision and together they exist as one global priesthood, under God and Rome. I came to learn all of this as I wandered the church, in search of meaning. The information I learned would stand to me, whilst I unconsciously searched out one truth, I found so many more thank God.

Maronite priests are the same as Catholic priest you know and speak with daily, locally. What makes the Maronite different from the Latin rite (the Catholic rite of the priesthood was the one that JJ belonged to), is that Maronite priests can be married.

Yousef today works as a married Catholic priest in Israel.

I came to know Yousef as we shared classes and always found a great and humble man in speaking to him.

After Maynooth, I moved to Europe for some time losing contact with some of those I had grown close to during those formative years in Maynooth, including Yousef.

Outside the homely walls of Maynooth, I needed to find a home. I settled nowhere but always looked up wide-eyed and mouth open as I stumbled upon a church or cathedral in a hidden, picturesque village in France, Croatia, Bosnia, Germany or Spain. There was still something familiar, something I had grown to appreciate, especially during the years at Maynooth, but what I recognised was not nurtured, it was somehow within my nature. I would examine local notices and pamphlets strewn upon an antique mahogany table, as old as the rustic priest who fumbled around the sacristy, clattering in the distance let me be. But then

I would have to leave, and the feeling of familiarity dissipated, like a shimmering heat on the horizon, a horizon I seemingly could never reach?

Four years after I left Maynooth, on what would have been JJ's 72nd birthday, I found out that I am the son of a Roman Catholic Priest. It was an l evening in May of 2011 when I connected all the dots that spelt out the word, Father.

By a fireside, examining his poetry collection, I recognised myself within the syntax. The familiarity of Maynooth, the warmth I found in the church, the years of my youth, the grief at his grave, the prayers he taught me, the grief I swallowed, "he was my father" I exclaimed. It was like two Lego bricks clicking together, at last, complete integration, *Silentium* lost out to the truth.

A tear fell upon my mother's cheek.

I knew, not only who JJ was, but most importantly, who I am and what I had been chasing all those years. I was chasing myself!

The fire warmed and resurrected life within me from the cool grip of death that had embraced many years previously.

Still, to this day, the effect of living within a secret makes itself known. I engage in physical activity and biosynthesis psychotherapy to honour that which is preverbal, which connects with foetal programming, mentioned earlier, to loosen the long-term effects of *Silentium* which haunt me.

> "Biosynthesis is an in-depth Relational Somatic Psychotherapy and Depth Psychology Oriented Psychotherapy which forges a link between somatic or body existence, psychological existence and spiritual essence. Biosynthesis represents a new approach in Somatic Psychotherapy." (Irish Institute for Biosynthesis., 2020)

This knowledge lit a fire within me!

Connecting my love of the Catholic Church with my childhood experience, I instinctively turned to the Catholic Church and to my former classmates, many of whom are now priests, to discuss in confidence, this news.

Connecting this experience with my heritage was enlightening. Looking back at my time at Maynooth, whilst I loved every minute of it, I was able to look at my ancestral heritage and recognise a trait perhaps that was present within my family that brought me there.

Connecting the ancestral dots, reaching out to some old classmates for support and pastoral care, I was warmly welcomed.

Ireland, when compared to the global Church, stands out in terms of responding to a scandal within the church.

Ireland has come through much in terms of church scandal, and our priests are pastorally attuned. In contrast, internationally, the same might not be said of priests, especially regarding this issue, the children of priests and religious.

Post-2011, in full knowledge I recognised that it is essential to be able to feel like you can talk openly about things when they trouble you, thus my reasoning to reach out to those whom I felt might understand, old classmates and clergy. This was a world I was familiar with and knew well since childhood. Initially scared of media or tabloid intrusion, I retreated to the peripheries, only to emerge with an excellent and trustworthy group of people whom I knew I could trust.

Whilst I was in no way troubled about being who I am, the expectancy of not being allowed to talk about who I am, or the thoughts of being disallowed to speak openly, disturbed me greatly. However, many encouraged me to keep my mouth shut. A contradiction emerged, the more I thought about it.

Reflecting on what I learned as a child being brought to mass alongside my time at Maynooth, it seemed that the social undertone of silence that surreptitiously nodded at me, regarding my priestly paternity was absolutely and categorically contrary to the prolife ethos of Catholicism. Benedict XVI came to my mind.

> "An 'adult' faith is not a faith that follows the trends of fashion and the latest novelty[.]" (His Eminence Card. Joseph Ratzinger., 2005)

Reflecting on what I learned as a child being brought to mass alongside my time at Maynooth, it seemed that the social undertone of silence that surreptitiously nodded at me, regarding my priestly paternity was absolutely and categorically contrary to the prolife ethos of Catholicism. Benedict XVI came to my mind.

> "An 'adult' faith is not a faith that follows the trends of fashion and the latest novelty [.]" (His Eminence Card. Joseph Ratzinger., 2005)

I discussed this statement with Fr. Vincent Twomey, a former doctoral student of Benedict. He agreed that in light of Benedict's statement, one should never stigmatise the children of the ordained owing to paternity in any form, since the Catholic faith precludes any form of disrespect or marginalisation toward children no matter how they are conceived, given that prolife equates respect of life from womb to tomb.

In this, stigma and *Silentium* ought to be considered a "trend" that must be stamped out.

Still, no priests spoke of this issue from the pulpit. Maynooth was kind, but the children of the ordained and religious were not on the syllabus, nor was the issue openly discussed in any other seminary. I realised a dichotomy poking its nose above the surface of society, and that dichotomy took the shape of a child of a priest or religious.

This dichotomy was encased in the bubble wrap of non-acknowledgement and within that deliberate ignorance are many more children, all buried.

Unless something changes, these children may emotionally choke, in the grave of *Silentium* and all for the goodness of the church; drastic change, it became clear, is needed.

How could the sacrifice of celibacy rest its hallowed head upon a pillow of children, who are moulded and pressurised by *Silentium* from birth? Surely its credibility as a tradition rests in God alone, not silenced children who are silence. None of it made sense.

The contradiction was apparent, and I could not leave it alone, it kept me awake at night.

I met with old classmates at fireplaces, on Skype, chatting down telephone lines that stretched across the world.

As I listened to their verbal struggles, I saw despair.

They wanted to fix this issue but perhaps didn't know how, since it predated them. Within that despair, lay the frail man and boy who had given himself for the priesthood, but the ministry no more perfected him than he perfected the priesthood.

I had yet to reach out to my old and dear friend, Yousef.

Beneath the apparent pretence lay a hidden world wherein children who sought truth were interminably gagged with silence masked as privacy.

They buried their anxiety among the dying flowers of their childhood. Though, as their soft tears cascaded down the petals of youth, I, like them - a silenced, numb wreck of a boy, in my mother's arms, confused by the muted grief that exploded within me, behind my closed lips and dry eyes- recognised my own inner child, trembling. Thus, I saw so many more, and we all needed help!

I knew, ironically, Catholicism was the answer to this centuries-old systemic process of what we now know as *Silentium* and the Moral Argument. These barbaric practices that promote silence, themselves contradict Catholicism and what it stands for. Yet silence remained around this issue? How could that be, how could Catholicism and *Silentium* exist?

I was discouraged from being open about my priestly heritage, I must confess, never by a man wearing a collar, but unnamed laity that will face God and I pray he is merciful toward them.

Indeed, "forgive them, for they do not know what they are doing," Jesus says. (Luke 23:34.)

I saw stigma and stared it in the face, and it woke me up.

I was naïve.

Whilst it irritated me at my core, I considered, what other option is there other than silence? Funnily enough, had I been left alone, I probably would not have opened my mouth.

> "I mean, no organisation dedicated toward fostering openness toward this phenomenon is in existence", I quietly contemplated in the months and year that followed the 2011 revelation about my biological father.

This was the germination of Coping.

It grew out of the manure of stigma, which conversely had the exact opposite effect of its intended aim. I find tremendous and Divine humour in that. Years upon years of research followed that afternoon in my county Longford childhood home.

As the sun shone through the glass window, from across the garden and fields where my father once walked with me, wherein he has lain for years entombed by nature and prayers, new life was emerging for so many, from the Philippines to Brazil and beyond.

My friends at Maynooth continued to be a source of friendship and support to me, among them, Yousef.

Yousef would prove to be a human confirmation, or validation, of the ability of a Catholic priest to parent, something my father could not do, without tremendous sacrifice, sacrificing me, I wanted to stop this cruel process.

Yousef proved to be instrumental to the formation of this organisation, Coping International, Children of Catholic Priests.

It is incredible who can be sitting beside you in your classroom, as you pen your thoughts and reach for academic greatness.

Your brother and sisters around you will form a part of your future, but you don't know it.

Yousef would unpack one of the most repetitive roadblocks I encountered over the years following 2011/2012 when Coping began to emerge.

There exists a misleading and harmful belief that Catholic priesthood and responsible paternity are mutually exclusive. I refer to this as the Impracticality Argument.

Something about celibacy as the years drifted on bothered me, not its existence, just the opposite. I never felt in my gut that calling for its abolition was the answer, yet it took time to sunder out why? Why not call for an absolute abolition of celibacy?

Simply put, people have called for the abolition of celibacy since it was introduced first centuries ago and it has not worked.

Secondly, I believe in picking your battles, and God knows, the chorus of "abolish celibacy" is loud enough without me adding another note to the already, abundant choir.

More importantly, if I suggest that adequate care provided toward the children of the ordained and religious is contingent upon the abolition of celibacy, I am indirectly suggesting that celibate (unmarried) priests are unable to care adequately for their offspring owing to the presence of celibacy.

This is akin to saying that unmarried men or women cannot care for children, which is untrue.

Thus, I would reinforce the argument that implies priests-fathers must leave ministry to provide for their child. In other words, I, in calling for the abolition of celibacy, ironically reinforce the alleged Impracticality Argument claimed by many of the hierarchy, including Cardinal Sepe, in 1993.

Lastly, if care toward children of priests is dependent upon the abolition of celibacy, I fear these children may starve.

The roadblock I speak of, the Impracticality Argument, is the recurring theme of the alleged divided heart of a priest, should he share his time between family and priesthood.

Cardinal Crescenzio Sepe, 1993 stated in 1993,

> "the married priest would be divided between two types of fruitfulness: that of the Church and that of marriage and bringing up children; and his own heart would bear the sign of division between love for the community and love for his family." (Sepe. C. C.)

I contacted Cardinal Sepe about his comments, but he simply replied,

> "I have no further comments on this matter."
>
> (Sepe. C. , 2020)

I believed if I am wrong, he would have contradicted me. This former statement made by His Eminence in 1993, typifies the recurrent argument that inhibits the progress of the married priest in the Latin rite and echoes the Moral Argument.

The priest would "bear [a] sign of division" it is claimed.

I disagree with this statement with every fibre of my being, because it is untrue from a Catholic perspective, regardless of my father's profession.

I believe that Cardinal Sepe's account is merely a linguistic argument that exists solely to convince people that priests and religious, cannot marry, be parents and priests/religious at the same time, owing to time and work commitments.

Though I cite His Eminence, it is a popularised belief held by many and not he alone.

The Impracticality Argument is profoundly problematic and misleading.

If priests and religious were not acting as parents and priests at the same time already, I would not be writing this book, and you certainly would not be reading about it. Secondly, Coping International would not exist either.

Lastly, the Vatican would not have released guidelines on the matter of children of priests in 2020, much less composed them.

Indeed, His Holiness Pope Benedict XVI would certainly not have agreed that "being a priest's [child] in no way can mean a burden or demerit for the [child]." (Cardinal Claudio Hummes, 2019).

The Irish Bishops would not have rightly and admirably, defended the natural rights of the children of the ordained, followed by more than a dozen international episcopal conferences who acted similarly if priests and religious were not priests, religious and parents simultaneously and inevitably.

Many have promoted the idea that Catholic priests cannot be parents and priests at the same time, a baseless logic. The Impracticality Argument fosters the Moral Argument, thus distancing the practice of consecrated chaste celibacy from procreative "lamentable defection". This undermines not only the child but celibacy itself from a sanctification perspective.

The priesthood seems to be the only job in the world where men and women automatically are expected to leave their employment to care for their child.

Usually, men who become parents seek increased security, not the other way around. The Impracticality Argument is disguised as a moral act, when, in fact, it is as noble as knowingly placing a parent in a situation of unemployment owing to paternity.

To me, it just does not add up.

At the heart of this proposition (the Impracticality Argument) is the intention of convincing society that Latin rite married priesthood is not possible pragmatically, that is the foundations of the Impracticality Argument, not child centeredness.

> "It is sometimes said that priests make a commitment to celibacy because the life of a priest is so busy that he would never be able to care for a family. It is true that priests are busy, but lots of other people are busy too. Many of these busy people are also good husbands and wives, fathers, or mothers. It is also true that many journalists, politicians, and doctors will say that their professional commitments *can* make it very difficult to have a normal family life. In reality, the reasons for celibacy are more symbolic than practical." (Diocese of Elphin.)

Thus, the Impracticality Argument is based on opinion, not Catholicism and certainly not doctrine.

Those who live a chaste and celibate (unmarried life), authentically, should be respected since they lived this life faithfully and choose this life openly and honestly.

Their sacrifice is real, and in the eyes of God should not be mocked or judged in the same way, one would not mock another person's prayer or lifestyle.

Just as secular society has not the right to condemn authentic celibacy, neither has the priesthood the right to undermine authentic chaste celibacy by associating this centuries-old tradition with abusive practises such as the Moral Argument to preserve norm and status. The celibate lifestyle in no way impinges upon the ability to parent neither does the job commitments affect the ability to parent.

The absolutist assumption of the priest's alleged inability to be a responsible parent, whilst working as priests/religious does not stand up, logically speaking. Many priests and religious remain secret about their paternity, since a child out of wedlock and a priest remaining in ministry, openly so, might be viewed as possibly sullying one's moral authority on a social level as a priest or religious. Hence, the alleged impracticality argument is wheeled out so frequently.

Given that the purported impracticality, divided heart argument lies at the apex of silence, *Silentium*, stepping aside from ministry into a very uncertain future, I turned to the Maronites to unpack this misleading and historic untruth, that is the Impracticality Argument.

The Maronite Catholic Church is part of the Catholic Church, under Roman rule and is what is referred to as a different rite, within the Catholic Church. I turned to them as I knew that Yousef was and is a married priest, a good priest. It made no sense that a Latin rite priest would bear a "sign of division" yet Yousef and those like him did not bear any such heaving theological burden given that all priests are the same?

I asked Cardinal Rahi a question in 2017. He is the Patriarch of the Maronites.

> "Can you, in your authority as Patriarch of Antioch and all the East of the Maronites, briefly describe the differences (if any) between a Latin rite Priest and a Maronite Priest in terms of his daily activity and priestly life; what does he

do (or not as the case may be) that a Latin rite Priest does (or does not as the case may be) which allows the Maronite Priest to be married and the Latin rite to not marry?" - Coping International, 2017.

His Eminence, Cardinal Rahi, kindly responded.

"As you said in your letter, some of our priests are married, and some are celibate. Both married and celibate Maronite priests do the same pastoral work. The Latin rite priests who are celibate do the same work as our celibate priests, and as our celibate and married priests have the same pastoral tasks, then, the logical conclusion is that both Latin priests who are celibate do the same pastoral work as the Maronite married priests." (al-Rahi, 2018)

Now, given that Maronite priests are the very same as your local Catholic priest, except for the tradition that says he can be married, the words "do the same pastoral work" should be resounding in your head by now. "Bear a sign of division", "moral obligation to step aside" stands in direct opposition to "[they] do the same pastoral work." Consequently, if the Maronites do the same as the unmarried priest, the tradition of being unmarried or celibate rests upon choice, not a practical necessity that requires it?

If Catholic priests were so busy that they could not openly have a wife and family (since some Latin rite Catholic priests do marry, in civil ceremonies, secretly), then celibacy would cease to be a choice, lessening its sacrificial nature. It would become a by-product of the job.

The sacrificial character of celibacy is contingent upon the ability to marry, but refusal to. To view celibacy in such simplistic terms would be disingenuous to those who authentically live it, which is unfair. So, celibacy does not exist because it must practically exist for the priesthood to function. Celibacy exists because the institution wishes it to exist not because it must, but some would like you to believe it is essential when it is in not.

Indeed, "the reasons for celibacy are more symbolic than practical." (Diocese of Elphin.)

However, whilst celibacy may be an excellent idea, spiritually speaking, pragmatically, it is problematic.

The tendency to hide that practical problem, the "lamentable defection", from which emanates, the children of the ordained, is both historic and popularised, and it wound up with *Silentium*.

Reflecting on the words of Cardinal Rahi, I recollected those days in Maynooth, staring out the windows onto the acreage of lush greenery as the sun caressed the grey and white stone walls of history, wherein prayers murmured and slipped off the quietened lips of ardent young men.

Once again, I remembered my friend, Yousef, the married priest in Israel.

I asked Yousef a question. His reply follows.

> "As a married Catholic priest, do you feel that your heart is divided between 'two types of fruitfulness', devotion to God and priesthood and devotion to family or, does one enrich the other for you?" – *Vincent Doyle*.

Haifa, Israel.

August 2020.

Via Email.

Dear Vincent,

Well done for choosing an especially important topic. Firstly, we believe in Father Son and Holy Spirit, its irony to say that the heart of the Father is divided because of His Only Son since God is "The Father." Thus, if we want to understand our God, then we must understand what fatherhood is about.

Unless celibate priests can bring their hearts to become a fatherly heart, they will remain far from the Father. The same as for the married priest if they cannot live out and bring their fatherhood to universal fatherhood, they cannot be a true fatherly priest.

So, whether the priests are unmarried or married, they both are called to this universal fatherhood.

I believe that it is easier for a married priest to understand what it means to be a father, as its part of his identity 24 hours.

He wakes up for many nights for his children as they mature. Hence, I think it comes to him naturally, and when he spiritualizes his fatherhood, then he actualizes what people call him - father.

On the other hand, if the celibate priest cannot interiorize what it means to be a father, then his ministry becomes a mere liturgical service far from fatherly spiritual service.

A married priest indeed has a more demanding effort to be done on every level, because he is a husband and a father. Yet, this effort if done with love, only helps him to develop the deep sense of his vocation to be a true shepherd to a larger flock. A married person who cannot live out a true love to his wife and children, will then also become an actor of 'liturgical service' rather than a 'liturgical father and servant'.

Finally, on a personal note, I am thankful to God for my wife and children; they are my everyday school of what it means to be a priestly father in the Church. Many times, I understood the various difficulties and suffering of families because I have a family.

Today, many priests lack this sense of being 24 hours for others and unfortunately their hearts maybe not divided but worse their heart is very cold to the degree that is almost not alive. The presence of the married priest along with celibate priest is the most precious gift to the Church. With mutual fatherly love between the celibate and married priest, then they reflect the beauty of the Church as one family that supports and challenges each other for good.

With many blessings,

Your brother in Christ,

Fr. Yousef Yakoub.

These words belonging to Yousef, genuinely reflect what it means to be a good Catholic, celibate priest, and a good, Catholic married priest.

The juxtaposition of the two quite clearly convey the reality that yes, the Catholic Church not only can allow, but already and traditionally has married and unmarried priests.

These traditions that differ need to immediately recognise, this difference in tradition, reinforcing this difference, psychologically divides the children of the ordained, who are conceived within a tradition where celibacy is mandatory, namely the Latin rite.

Not allowing the reality of children of priests within the Latin rite, to breathe, socially speaking is an act that cannot be interpreted as being fatherly, spiritually, or otherwise.

> "Unless celibate priests can bring their heart to become a fatherly heart, they will remain far from the Father."
>
> – Fr. Yousef Yakoub.

This is reminiscent of Pope Francis' words concerning fatherhood.

> "When a man does not have this desire, something is missing, something is wrong.'" (Pope Francis., 2013)

A true priest would recognise that a priest and biological father are a part of the Catholic Church, always have and always will be. God designed it so. A true shepherd would grace this situation with the compassion it deserves, not legislate it with orders and stringent mechanisms that promote unemployment and poverty. What is fatherly about forcing every father, every parent, automatically into a position of uncertainty, unemployment and all that goes with insecurity and unemployment, when the priest/religious becomes a parent?

> "A married priest indeed has a more demanding effort to be done on every level, because he is a husband and a father. Yet, this effort if done with love, only helps him to develop the deep sense of his vocation to be a true shepherd to a larger flock." – Fr. Yousef Yakoub.

To state that a priest would have a divided heart because he is a parent, is thus, misleading since thousands of priests are parents and priests simultaneously. Equally, it is insulting to all married clergy everywhere, so the roots of the Impracticality Argument rest in ego and opinion only, and untruth.

Love conjoins celibacy and priesthood just as love merges marriage, family, and ministry. Marriage and priesthood are not mutually exclusive. Whilst this may reduce the uniqueness of priesthood in some eyes, it introduces hope for the children conceived within the Latin rite priesthood, in the future.

These experiences, Maynooth, communicating with Cardinal Rahi and his sentiments which were buoyed by my friend Yousef would lead me to Rome, to the Congregation for Clergy.

Meetings at the Vatican are strangely ordinary and not at all what one might anticipate having been heavily influenced by media and film depictions of the Holy See.

Coping matured like wine over the successive years and remained insistent on gaining an audience with these departments.

I was relentless.

The Vatican granted these audiences and meetings when the data Coping presented, non-identifiable in nature, was made available to these various departments. This data that accumulates daily.

This was sufficient to convince them that knowledge existed confirming that a problem was being hidden, an issue that had bubbled to the surface, after been hidden for centuries, one of the oldest issues of the institutional Catholic Church.

A meeting was set for January 2020 with the Congregation.

I found myself back in Dublin airport, early morning, returning to Rome as I had done so many times before, only to knock on closed doors. This time, I had an invite.

Climbing the many stairs to the second floor of this Vatican office in Rome, I was hopeful. The rooms are ornate, expansive, and usually tiled. A picture of the Holy Father customarily adorns the wall facing the chair you are brought to. The door is routinely closed as you wait.

I examined the habitual coffee-table book of images of beautiful statues in Rome, many within the Vatican itself, as I awaited the persons that I was scheduled to meet. It is nice to hear the melodic Italian tone echoing in the next room, falling into the quietness of anticipation wherein my considerations ruminate. I consider, 'why I am here', 'how do I make the most of this time here?'

I am usually warm, not nervous, but one man moving in and around the Vatican accompanied with data, hope and water can take its toll on all 5'7 of me. I hang my head, hands joined in prayer and thought, as my shoes stare back up at me. What I am about to do circles my head.

To query the Vatican on their practices regarding the children that nobody knew they had to begin with, in the quantities that Coping is eliciting daily. Is this truly happening?

Before the meeting, I sat on the balcony of Residenza Paolo VI, a hotel that flanks the left colonnade of the Vatican drinking a coffee. Residenza Paolo VI is a hotel I frequent owing to its proximity to the Vatican on business trips to Rome.

The hotel balcony is on the same level as the 'loggia', the famous balcony, that the Holy Father famously walks onto after a new pope is elected and the famous words, *"Habemus papam"* echo across the world media.

As I stared at that historic balcony, the words *"Habemus papam"* ("we have a pope") echoed in my head. I thought of how close to history I was.

How one man can ask one question of the Holy See and how can one answer -however theologically rhetorical that question may be- like a mustard seed, and move mountains?

The mountain I need to move, or at least, begin to chip at, pre-exists us all. This mountain is a psychosocial expectation that no Latin rite priest/religious will ever retain the title, Father, as a priest whilst acknowledging his fatherhood, as a parent, at the same time. This unwritten rule is, as the saying goes, "as old as tea." It was time for a new pot to brew.

As my coffee encircled the bottom of the beautifully ornate china, I looked upon an ecclesiological tribute to time itself, centuries of Catholicism and society surrounded me. I speculated how many other children of priests have stared upon these walls and statues wondering is there a way out from beneath the heaving burden imposed upon them. Slowly, I made my way across *Via Della Conciliazione*, climbing the memorable and continual steps, murmuring prayers, as I had done by his grave, hoping for an answer.

I have never encountered resistance to realism regarding the children of the ordained in the Congregation for Clergy; it is outside these walls where misdirection exists and persists.

As I sat awaiting my hosts at that meeting in Rome, I reflected upon the Theology at Maynooth. Being connected to children of priests globally, the fact that married priests and unmarried priests do the same work, as has been confirmed by the Catholic Church. Slowly all three combined and pointed toward a twofold solution. Firstly, to allow men to remain in ministry -if they are parents- in certain circumstances, as opposed to fostering unemployment. Secondly, looking into the long-term, married clergy, *Viri Probati*, which I will examine in further detail in the next chapter.

Regarding this two-point plan, it must be recognised that a celibate, unmarried priest can care for a child, adequately, since one does not have to be married to be a good parent.

Whilst, having a loving, married mom and dad is the ideal, it is not realistic to expect this to happen always.

Thus, one must respond to the phenomenon of the children of the ordained practically, not idealistically with baseless sentiment underlined by false theology. Ideals do not feed children.

The door handle moves. I lift my gaze to the view of two priests, as pristine as if they had just walked out of seminary. Greetings are cordial and genuine. We all want this issue resolved in as best a manner as possible.

My tolerance of the Catholic Church institution perhaps emanates from its humanness, the men, and women that I meet did not themselves create the problem. They did not directly or indirectly neglect a child and are willing to help. So, I give them the dignity of listening to their suggestions on how to "remedy" the situation? (Pope Saint Paul VI., 1967.)

Pleasantries exchanged, the meeting in January 2020 at the Vatican, as it had done the year previous at the Vatican Sex Abuse Summit, begins with an outlay of questions, alongside a promise to put into writing, the results of what was discussed.

In that small room, where two Irishmen and one Italian, all seeking an answer to a controversial topic, conversed, we got to the heart of the matter quickly and definitively.

The impracticality argument circled my head that afternoon at the Vatican. It is the bullwhip that drives children of the ordained and their families into a future of uncertainty.

The dialogue that arose in that meeting that fateful January afternoon primarily concerned the Vatican Guidelines for the Children of Priests firstly made available to me in Geneva in 2017, and subsequently released following that same meeting in January 2020.

When confronted with the issue of priests remaining in ministry to "avert" the "wound" of unemployment, housing issues and so forth, the Vatican referenced the 2009 guidelines. (Pope Saint Paul VI., 1967.)

The Holy See clarified the third guideline relating to consolidated families in the addendum the Vatican guidelines mentioned previously.

This directly contradicts the earlier cited argument of the Impracticality Argument, as the Vatican permit exceptions, thus *ad hoc*, not in every case or indeed citing improbable impossibility.

The Addendum drove a stake through the heart of the clericalist barrier that underlines the absolutist nature of the Impracticality Argument. I happily welcomed it.

The Impracticality Argument, as well as being misleading, confines God as dependent upon a priesthood that expels those who become parents. This is theologically absurd.

Following this confirmation, that a priest can remain, the Italian Vatican official uttered the words of the Gospel of John (16:12), having reflected upon the conversation of when to tell a child, this to me was memorable.

> "... I have much more to say to you, more than you can now bear." John, 16:12.

I imagined these same words later upon the dying lips and heart of my late father.

We had discussed in that Vatican meeting, the weight of what it means to be the child of a priest or religious and the importance of ensuring the child can receive this information emotionally and psychologically.

To link this with the scripture, for me, was beautiful. I agreed that this specific scripture reference was wonderfully appropriate. It captures the genuine difficulties that are attached to the phenomenon of being the child of a Catholic priest. The Vatican agreed, the silence surrounding this issue can and is destructive. However, discernment as to when to tell the child will vary from case to case and will change within varying contexts and cultures, hence the Gospel verse, John 16:12.

Now a new issue presented, normalising this situation to the point that a priest could and would hold the hand of his son or daughter and walk down the street as a reconfirmed, celibate, chaste Catholic priest, a reality that the Vatican said was now possible.

I am grateful for the kindness offered to me by the Congregation for the Clergy. Nevertheless, episcopal conferences worldwide need to actualise this teaching that occurred that day, and indeed the Pope himself needs to say it aloud so all of history can hear it.

No bishop can credibly stand up and say that a parent who does not wish to marry, does not have the natural right, to walk down the street holding the hand of his child as a confirmed priest/religious and do so with honour, dignity and deserving of respect.

One priest who came to Coping, now married with a child, who was a former provincial of a well-known religious order confirmed to me, following the success of the January 2020 meeting, he wishes to remain anonymous.

> "The difficulty lies not in allowing the man to own his paternity whilst remaining a chaste and celibate priest, the difficulty lies in promoting the life of celibacy to young seminarians, whilst simultaneously older priests own their paternity, thus diminishing the value of celibacy."

This insight is the beating, living truth veiled behind the Moral Argument. It is crucial to recognise that, at the heart of the many issues that surround and drown the children of the ordained is the defence of the credibility of mandatory celibacy, not celibacy itself. As Pope Saint Paul VI stated, "the responsibility falls not on consecrated celibacy in itself." (Pope Saint Paul VI., 1967.)

Whilst the Holy See confirmed in their Vatican guidelines, exceptions allowing priests to remain in ministry having fathered a child, having this actualised globally is a different matter altogether. The Impracticality Argument had to be replaced, no matter how long this took. It had to die, a quick and sudden death, since it was and remains to be, a destructive element within so many families globally and historically manipulating its nature to appear as being child-centred when it is not.

Returning home, the Vatican confirmed that a priest may remain in the priesthood, having fathered a child, openly acknowledge his child, and recommit to chastity and celibacy.

What I term, *Parēns* became a reality.

Parēns refers to the situation where a Latin Rite priest who becomes a parent, latterly recommits to celibacy and chastity, whilst simultaneously openly acknowledging his biological child, as he continues to work as a celibate, chaste Roman Catholic, Latin rite priest.

Parēns, Latin for 'parents', 'ancestors', is a much better response to priestly paternity than the Moral Argument, a by-product of which is *Silentium*. *Parēns* in part addresses the untruth the Impracticality Argument promulgates, but not fully. Now that a third term has been introduced, it is helpful to recap on the three terms discussed thus far.

1. **Silentium** refers to the process of silencing a child of an ordained person/religious concerning the child's identity as the child of an ordained person/religious.

2. **The Moral Argument**, the unceasing and unyielding claim that a priest/or religious must leave the ministry if he or she becomes a parent.

3. **Parēns** refers to the situation where a Latin rite priest, recommits to celibacy and chastity, whilst openly

acknowledging his biological child, as he continues to work as a celibate, chaste Roman Catholic, Latin rite priest.

Examining the three terms, one can see the link between the three. *Silentium* is a by-product of the Moral Argument (which is nurtured by the Impracticality Argument). *Parēns*, however, does not necessitate *Silentium* and allows priests/religious to continue to work as a priest/religious, designated as "not impossible", thus possible, by the Vatican.

It would be insincere not to recognise that a priest who has had sex, fathered a child, and not married the mother of his child may evoke hypocrisy and critics of *Parēns*, may do well to highlight this hypocritical situation. However, we know priests and religious are flawed and human. We see that they are sinful. This is not news. It is hypocritical to continue to foster and encourage a systemic process knowingly, that insists, all priests and religious must leave ministry having become a parent. Thus, hypocrisy is inevitable. Thus, our intent must always be to protect children, and the Moral Argument does not do that. Whilst

Parēns may, for some, mean highlighting behaviour deemed as scandalous, what is disgraceful, is scandalising a child.

The Moral Argument thus is the height of hypocrisy as it does not indicate employment or housing options post ministry. A priest who has a child can openly acknowledge his flawed humanity before God and man, and any moral uncertainty indeed can be responded to with love, as Fr. Yakoub confirmed.

> "If paternity and priesthood are 'done with love, it only helps him to develop the deep sense of his vocation to be a true shepherd to the larger flock.'"

That afternoon in the Vatican, as the world passed by, three men sat quietly and considered matters that are difficult to handle. It struck me as we sat there, we are all young men, three sons ourselves (only one priest's son), nonetheless, served with sundering out a centuries-old problem. It was as staggering as it was simple, do not fire the parent. It was honestly that simple, and if his or her (in the case of female religious) resignation from the ministry is imminent, you have a moral duty to go beyond baseless sentiment, to actualising that which you say.

If she is a nurse, let her be a nurse. If he is a teacher, let him teach. Do not take away his spoon that he feeds his child with one hand, whilst with the other upon your heart, advise him/her to fulfil their moral obligation.

That evening in January 2020 it was agreed, parents could watch their children grow up, openly and without fear of reprisal, unemployment, homelessness or worse, watching their children suffer from emotional and psychological neglect arising from *Silentium*. Maybe now children would not grow hungry, emotionally, physically, psychologically or otherwise.

The realisation and allowance and acknowledgement that it is now, "not impossible" for a priest to be a parent, openly so, is the first step toward achieving transparency surrounding priestly and religious paternity. But much remains to be done.

So *Parēns* is step one and is in part achieved but needs actualisation. Step two, *Viri Probati*, is the answer in the long term. This will be discussed in the next chapter.

Parēns, step one, nurtures and comes before step two, *Viri Probati*, married priests. Both *Parēns* and *Viri Probati* presume one-another and categorically eliminate the Moral Argument.

Where once we had the Impracticality Argument and the Moral Argument, now we propose and lay claim to *Parēns* and *Viri Probati* in its place.

As I reflect upon that young boy of twenty-one years of age, wandering the priestly halls of Maynooth, unwittingly, little did I know that God would lead me to Rome and into the hearts of hidden people.

I thought of the kids to come, inevitable children of the ordained. They must not endure what we have suffered from, we the historical children of the ordained and religious, as well as our parents.

Thus, I persevere, but not just for these children, but for Catholicism itself, founded upon the back of a rejected child born to a frightened girl.

Chapter Five.

Viri Probati.

Pope Saint Paul VI once commented,

> "Celibacy 'cannot be abandoned or subjected to argument."
>
> (Pope Saint Paul VI, 1970)

Celibacy is privately "subjected to argument" each time a Catholic priest breaks his vow of chastity or indeed when he marries in secret.

His Holiness Pope Saint Paul VI recognised this very point when he referred to the "lamentable defection", referring to priests and religious who have sexual relations, in 1967.

Thus, his statement might read more correctly if he stated, which he most certainly did not,

"Celibacy 'cannot be abandoned or subjected to argument, out loud, but inevitably will be contravened, inevitably, in private."

The notion of a married priesthood has been bandied about since it became traditional that priests remain celibate, meaning unmarried, however married clergy is not unknown in the Catholic world.

"Married priests are permitted in the eastern Catholic rites, and one of Benedict's central goals is full communion with the Orthodox. Anglican priests, married or not, are already permitted to become Catholic priests, but on a case-by-case basis. The new dispensation would for the first time allow in groups of married priests" (Donadio., 2009)

Men leaving Latin rite ministry to get married is not uncommon or unheard of.

However, could these men return to priestly ministry as married priests?

I asked Archbishop Paul-Nabil Sayah, Archbishop of the Maronite Archeparchy of Haifa and the Holy Land the following question.

"Would the Maronite church be opposed to applications for priestly formation of men, who requested dispensation from the Latin rite, having fathered a child and left to marry, but still feel a calling to priestly ministry?"

The Archbishop kindly and inspiringly replied.

"Up to recently Rome and the local Latin rite bishops never agreed, as you know, to allow Eastern Catholic married clergy to serve in parishes located within their jurisdiction. Now that they do, I feel one could be justified in putting the question to one of the Eastern rite Catholic bishops there. Because of the shortage of vocations, an Eastern Catholic bishop may be willing, in theory, to consider such a person for ministry. However, the case has to be referred back to Rome, as only the Holy Father, who laicised the priest, i.e. suspended him of his priestly functions, (an ordained priest is a priest forever) could restore those functions back. God's mercy and forgiveness being infinite would not, in my opinion, allow one mistake to ruin the whole life and vocation of an otherwise good and devoted priest, thus depriving the Church of a very valid ministry. Having said that, I feel that Rome would be very reluctant to create such [a] precedent for very obvious reasons."

(Archbishop Paul-Nabil Sayah, 2020)

Thus, men who leave ministry to marry in the Latin rite may consider returning to ministry within the Eastern tradition with the permission of His Holiness, and the local bishop, as a married man. Thus, journalists must ask the Pope this question.

> "Would His Holiness permit such a move (Laicised Latin rite priest to married Eastern rite priest), if such a move was for the good of that family, as agreed by the family and respective bishop, even on an *ad hoc* basis?"

If indeed, "God's will is rarely to be found in merely seeking out what is most palatable for those on the inside", (McKeown., 2020) will His Holiness allow a Latin to Eastern rite movement, of a laicised priest, if the priest-father is a good priest and a devoted and loving father?

Men should not have to choose between family and/or the priesthood when neither one contradicts the other.

If the priest father's employment perspectives are low to non-existent outside of ministry, and if he is an "otherwise good and devoted priest," then, would a sitting Pope reinstate the priest's faculties in these circumstances, or would he maintain the tradition of not doing so further enabling economic neglect?

Celibacy has always been divisive, politically speaking.

Like opposing teams, some hold in high esteem the tradition of celibacy, whilst others refer to it as antiquated, unworkable, or inhuman.

I feel that if someone chooses to be celibate and chaste and offer that up to God if someone is unmarried and is authentically offering this as a sacrifice, then who am I to judge him?

Even if I did not believe in God, even if I was an atheist, who am I to judge him, in what he feels is appropriate to offer up to God the Father?

In 2020, the Vatican made a statement about former religious leaving ministry, and the statement mentioned priests and religious who fall in love.

"'Today, fidelity is fluid, and the crisis consecrated life faces is the same one experienced within families.' With this affirmation, [Vatican Archbishop] José Rodríguez Carballo describes the context of one reality of the Church: that of religious men and women abandoning consecrated life. According to the secretary of the Vatican department for religious institutes, in 2019, 1,600 people left the consecrated life. He says this is due to three main causes: faith crises, community life crises and affective crises. [...] 'This is what's commonly presented as the main cause. A religious man falls in love with a woman. A religious woman falls in love with a man. Well, it's a fact. However, we have to see why and how it's come to this. It's come to this, in many cases, because of a lack of a concrete, real faith, because of a lack of profound fraternity." (Rome Reports., 2020)

His Excellency's statement is important, but it must be recognised that fidelity has always been fluid. The only difference is the absence of fidelity is discovered more easily now. Nothing has changed. Fidelity has always been fluid.

His Excellency asks, "why and how it's come to this?" Religious life and priesthood have always been like this.

This is not new.

Priesthood and religious life assume human nature.

Thus, the priesthood is expressed humanly, not robotically or automatically.

Sacrifice assumes a degree of failure or possibility thereof.

Consequently, priests and religious breaking celibacy and chastity will remain a real part of the Catholic priesthood into the future, because "fidelity [was,] is [and always will be] fluid."

One can no more inhibit a physical expression of human sexuality within the celibate and chaste priesthood and religious life than one can stop the tide from flowing. It is a part of human life and thus, is inevitable whether you are a priest, religious or layperson.

One thousand six hundred people left religious life in 2019 alone.

The question remains, how many did not and yet perhaps should have left, according to the belief of some?

How many then live in total silence about their children?

If 1600 have been upfront, leaving the ministry, how many were not upfront?

Moreover, of that 1600, how many had a real choice?

"1600 people left religious."

Was the choice to leave voluntary, or did it follow a prolonged period of suspension denoted as a discernment period?

Coping has seen this time and time again; a priest fathers a child and then is advised to take a leave of absence, denoted as a time to reflect. Periods of discernment are often extended to the point where it becomes inevitable the man is never returning, forgotten and the world moves on.

If half of the 1600, annually, for the previous nine years depart, that indicates thousands leaving the priesthood and religious life in the past decade alone.

This is global, then what of these families, post-ministry, in contexts where Catholicism is socially ingrained. Are they Coping?

It is clear to see why the issues surrounding children of priests and religious are preferred by many to remain, unacknowledged, reflecting on these numbers. This raises an eyebrow as to the real number. This real and rising number was created over a century and not overnight.

If falling in love is the "main cause" for priests and religious leaving ministry, how many dishonest religious remain silent, and consequently, so too their children?

Considering these figures, juxtaposing them with the statistics accumulated by Coping International since 2014, data which accrues daily, what is the correct procedure in responding to this reality if the Moral Argument, is inadequate?

What is *Viri Probati?*

> "The expression, *Viri Probati* is inspired from the first-century letter of a disciple of the apostles, St. Clement. [...] The idea is that in situations of extreme lack of priests, married people with 'proven' fidelity to the Catholic Church could be ordained [to the Catholic Priesthood.]."
>
> (Rome Reports., 2017)

To say that the idea has generated much controversy would be an understatement.

In 2019, Pope Francis called a synod, which is essentially an assembly of clergy gathered to discuss matters affecting the Church, or social issues of importance.

The Amazonia Synod occurred in 2019.

At the Synod, the issue of *Viri Probati* was discussed at length, and many hoped this would mark the beginning of married priests.

The Holy See commented.

> "Some Synod Fathers have raised the question of ordaining married men, *Viri Probati*, valuing what may be in time the validity of such an experience." (Synod.va, 2019)

Does this mean the Catholic Church is considering abolishing celibacy? Should celibacy remain? Whether celibacy remains or whether celibacy is abolished, is irrelevant when considering the phenomenon of the children of the ordained, since priests and religious, like members of secular society, are going to have sex outside of wedlock and children will result, regardless. Similarly, unmarried people can care for the children they create outside of wedlock, so marriage from a care perspective is not the automatic or only answer.

Focusing on the abolition of celibacy, as stated, suggests that celibates cannot care for children. However, a second problem arises, often cited by critics of the abolition of celibacy, infidelity within a marriage.

Whilst marriage may never remedy marital infidelity, neither will celibacy eradicate celibate and clerical chaste infidelity.

Thus, infidelity is the problem, not absolutes, marriage and celibacy. The origins of the problems we experienced are human-based.

Nevertheless, if we embrace these absolutes, so too, we must embrace their direct counterparts, marital and celibate infidelity as fidelity and infidelity assume one another, humanly speaking. Consider, if celibacy were abolished tomorrow, would all priests remain faithful to their wives forever and a day? The Anglican situation mentioned confirms the answer to this is likely to be no; they would not all remain faithful. It is doubtful to assume all men who are married, would always stay loyal to their wives, though, one expects that most would be faithful.

Post-ministerial employment may be difficult to find in the situation where a priest is forced out of his position owing to infidelity. Thus, clerical infidelity is not unique to a celibate clergy. This issue is familiar to Catholicism as well as other Christian Churches and Denominations.

What the Anglican phenomenon proves, to whatever degree, is that infidelity does not cease when men marry, secular society tells us that every day.

A father who is a married priest might have an affair but is this is not a reason to stop children of the ordained and religious of the future experiencing life within a family context because some may mess things up.

If potential marital infidelity is a solid argument for refusing married clergy because of the possible indiscretions of some, then would celibacy as a tradition not cease owing to the indiscretions of some clergy and religious consequently?

Some have used the infidelity argument to hinder the progress of married clergy when, in fact, it equally undermines celibacy also. The assertion that married clergy should not be permitted because they may be unfaithful incredibly whitewashes over the fact that celibate and chaste clergy are disloyal to the celibate and chaste life. Married clergy should be allowed as a response to inevitable children that will be fathered by allegedly chaste and celibate priests.

> "In my experience as a priest and as a bishop, the instance of when a priest has fathered a child has not been very frequent." (Cardinal Sean O'Malley, 2017)

I have great respect for Cardinal O'Malley. However, respectfully, given that, a priest or religious who fathers a child is unlikely to tell his brother priests, much less his bishop about his newfound paternity. Thus, this statement would read more accurately, in my opinion, if His Eminence stated the following, (which he did not to my knowledge).

> "In my experience as a priest and as a bishop, the instances of priests fathering children has not been frequent. However, in all probability, some conceptions of children of the ordained may pre-exist my priesthood and time. Thus, exact numbers are unknown to the wider Church and me if truth be told, and this is true of the entire, collective Church, globally speaking."

The argument that condemns the notion of married clergy and efforts at minimising the phenomenon of the children of the ordained are two arguments that are baseless in reason and are juxtaposed. It is important to highlight them, remember them, question them, undermine them and ultimately, remove them.

Consider how many priests have been ordained since 1938 worldwide, 79 years ago? Of that number of men ordained to the priesthood, how many were neither chaste nor celibate throughout their ministry? How many pregnancies resulted? Thus, many pregnancies would logically pre-exist the sitting bishop leaving him, entirely in the dark, through no fault of his own. This precludes grandchildren of priests where the adult child of a priest/religious is deceased.

I often speak with children of priests and religious who are older than the sitting bishop/provincial/superior. Thus, ignorance as to the real numbers is not a clerical failure, rather a by-product of the nature of this issue as historic.

Children of priests occur over time, albeit steadily and incessantly. The actual number of children balloons when one reflects historically speaking because this issue can't be stopped, ever.

Priests fathering children is certainly not a thing of the past, it continues to present to Coping today and, in all probability, will long into the future.

What is happening now will likely present itself in twenty years also. What happened regarding chaste clerical obedience over the past century is a part of the presenting phenomenon today, regarding the children of the ordained and so on.

This is the nature of this issue, and what makes it complicated even more so is the fruit of the act is a new human being that can speak for itself.

The tendency to lessen the blow, to dumb down the phenomenon is exceedingly popular, minimalizing this issue is a by-product of the reality of non-acknowledgement discussed in chapter one, which is the main problem, to begin with.

Curbing of this issue keeps the whole issue at bay and with it, those who believe that they are the only one, the only child of a priest/religious.

Minimising this issue feeds social non-acknowledgement of the children of the ordained, who in their very person, "demonstrate

the finitude and the limits of even the most sublime vocation."
(Ferrarotti, 2020)

Ferrarotti further notes,

> "the children of priests are in fact the living proof of human sinfulness and at the same time the testimony of a biblical promise that has not been kept." (Ferrarotti, 2020)

These children, it is wrongly believed, must be kept at bay.

What other scandal in the Catholic Church refuses to die and is carried on within DNA intergenerationally in the absence of a child?

If a crime is committed by a priest or religious against another person, if that same victim never discloses this crime, knowledge of the offence will likely die with the victim, unfortunately.

Children of priests as adults become parents, and thus the DNA of the priests becomes a living witness to clerical indiscretion, regardless of how long ago it happened.

DNA and genealogy, like an archaeologist tenderly scraping back the years with a brush, unwraps sexual indiscretions decades after the fact.

The fact that celibacy is impossible to quantify stands in direct contrast to the fact that one can quantify its palpable absence, via DNA. Consequently, owing to the inevitability of the procreative "lamentable defection", if celibacy is to remain, then *Viri Probati* must begin if children are to be protected and celibacy is to be realistically and increasingly authentic, spiritually and humanly speaking.

How are *Viri Probati* and the phenomenon of the children of the ordained connected?

Is *Viri Probati,* not a response to dwindling priestly numbers?

Yes, *Viri Probati* is indeed a suggested response to dwindling priestly vocations and a lack of priests in certain regions. However, it has an unintended effect.

Young men who present for the priesthood, owing to *Viri Probati* could discern their call to live a chaste and celibate life, earlier, as opposed to discovering their apparent inability or unwillingness as they stare into an incubator that holds their secret child as a middle-aged priest.

As an alternative to becoming a celibate priest, they marry, have a wife and children whilst nurturing the interior priestly vocation within this context.

In this, we would echo the Maronite tradition.

I am reminded of Yousef's words.

> "The presence of the married priest along with celibate priest is the most precious gift to the Church."

Thus, juxtaposing the two via *Viri Probati* is a gift, not a sign of contradiction. However, how is this beneficial? Primarily, all discerning seminarians cannot choose celibacy.

It is selected for them, centuries ago, as part of what they discern. You cannot discern priesthood minus celibacy, which is sad.

Thus, their celibate and chaste strength is a lifelong effort. The Vatican commented as follows.

> "The pilgrim Church on earth must strive daily to ensure optimum priestly formation that will prepare future sacred ministers to faithfully live their total consecration, bearing in mind that grace builds on nature and that priestly formation is an ongoing journey that continues through the whole of life." (Congregation for Clergy, 2020)

Lying at the border of this "sublime vocation" are children of the ordained.

This has always been the reality of the Catholic priesthood and it unavoidably always will be. How can something so innocent, a child, be painted as something so negative whose conception is considered by some as "lamentable"?

Thus, should the inevitability of clerical paternity be expressed within a marriage in advance of ordination having discerned, carefully, one's call to the celibate life or not, as the case may be? I believe it is selfish, heartfully selfish to prohibit *Viri Probati* for adult centered reasons.

A church without *Viri Probati* limits opportunities for the inevitable children of the ordained, to be born into families, not laden with nor anticipative of stigma, marginalisation, societal banishment and harm.

The church must anticipate these children's existences and cater to them in advance. What children need, not what adults want should always be prioritised. Surely this should be the first call of the Catholic priesthood.

If the child abuse scandal has taught nothing else, it is that children come first.

Viri Probati coexisting with celibate priests would almost altogether eliminate phenomena such as *Silentium* alongside the Moral Argument.

Whilst I recognise that infidelity can occur within clerical marriage, as the Anglican context attests to, this is not a viable reason to not furnish children of the ordained of the future with a stable domestic environment, supported by *Parēns*, with a specific focus on guidelines three and four of the Vatican guidelines.

In exceptions where celibate priests did father a child in the future, in a Church where *Viri Probati* is an actualised reality, then that would be dealt with on a case by case basis, as per Vatican Guidelines, keeping the good of the child at the heart of all action taken, cognisant of *Parēns*.

The young prospective seminarian in a situation where *Viri Probati* is actualised could discern his calling in advance of the priesthood. In this, celibacy would truly radiate as a brilliant jewel, truly and openly chosen, within the brotherhood of the Catholic clergy, as opposed to being a family heirloom passed on.

If the Catholic Church truly valued and held celibacy in high esteem, it would allow young men to choose to either offer up one's life as a celibate, or discern priesthood as a married man, and offer that richness to God's priesthood alongside his celibate brothers and sisters.

If celibacy were genuinely respected by the institutional Catholic Church, protection of this gem would not be contingent upon enslaving families to the Moral Argument and *Silentium*.

The human person is worth more than this and so too, the tradition of celibacy.

If celibacy is of God, then man has wrecked what was once a brilliant jewel, linking it with the Moral Argument, itself conjoined with *Silentium*.

However, many are vehemently against the implementation of *Viri Probati*.

Arguments against its application usually centre around the law of celibacy.

"If you weaken the law of celibacy, you open a breach, a wound in the mystery of the Church" according to Cardinal Robert Sarah. (Cardinal Robert Sarah., 2020)

These words were said by a Vatican Cardinal in 2020.

It appears that he considers *Viri Probati* a means by which celibacy would be weakened.

I understand where he is coming from, I disagree with him, but I understand his position.

From the church's position, celibacy is their offering, a gift, a sacrifice, something of love given to God. Amending celibacy in their eyes is tarnishing a gift that costs so much.

However, consider the implementation of *Viri Probati* from another angle.

What use is this priceless "jewel" of celibacy if it is protected to the degree where children are harmed via the Moral Argument and *Silentium*?

Would God want this gift then? Does celibacy's mandatory nature please Him, given that the mandatory nature of celibacy endorses the Moral Argument and indeed, *Silentium* too?

If mandatory celibacy is abolished in the morning, a man or woman could still choose to be celibate and offer up their lives as a celibate, unmarried person if they wished.

Thus, what *Viri Probati* weakens is not celibacy intrinsically, but its present mandatory nature just as marriage does not weaken the vocation to the single life.

Maintaining the mandatory nature of celibacy in conjunction with the conveyor belt of forced priestly resignation for those who father children (the Moral Argument), is profoundly selfish.

The absolutist nature of chaste celibacy marginalises those who are neither chaste nor celibate and their children also which is deeply sad. Consider the following.

1. If priests being married weakens celibacy, then what do priests having sex while still pretending to be chaste and celibate, do to celibacy? I imagine nothing good. Thus, if His Eminence is right, celibacy then, by his logic, is already in such a profoundly weakened state that it may be past rescuing owing to "lamentable defection" as recognised by Pope Saint Paul VI in 1967.

2. It could be argued that celibacy is no more weakened by married clergy, than a man/woman who chooses to be single and unmarried is impaired in their choice, by another who wants marriage. If they are happy in their choice to be single, then the opposite choice will likely reinforce, or not affect, their initial decision, not weaken it.

3. Why does celibacy have to be collectively strong? Why mandatory? Celibacy is individual, is it not? Moreover, celibacy is unquantifiable. Thus, how does one strengthen an unquantifiable, individualistic tradition? Therefore, it is the image and credibility of celibacy that is preserved - by keeping *Viri Probati* at bay- not individual actualisation of celibacy.

There exists a lot of baseless linguistic hyperbole around the phenomenon of celibacy.

If you break it down to nuts and bolts, you have this; all Catholics are called to be chaste, priests and religious promise to remain celibate, though, not all stay celibate nor chaste. For the everyday Catholic, we have reconciliation, yet for the priest and religious, they have apology and suspension and expulsion.

Is this of God or man? If it is of man and it is for God, then does God want this and if not, why do we force it upon Him?

Perhaps then it is neither of or for God and just of man and for certain men only.

If this is the case, then, this is greed, a wolf in sheep's clothing of immorality. Expelling priestly and religious parents based on an alleged intention of goodness for the child, without a clue as to how the parent may achieve this, especially in developing countries, is gravely wrong.

Furthermore, be warned, a subjective argument of positive stories of so-called, former priests and religious post-ministry, in no way counteracts the objective reality, of the presenting and pervasive reality of the Moral Argument, which itself, at least in part (to whatever degree) fosters unemployment, suffering and desolation.

If celibacy remains and *Viri Probati* is not introduced, celibacy is still weak, as it is dependent on finite human nature.

More celibates no more increase obedience to celibacy, than an increased marriage rate would enhance spousal fidelity.

Fidelity is individual, not collective.

Some might hold that *Viri Probati* diminishes celibacy to being considered of being of lesser value.

However, in whose eyes is celibacy reduced, God or man?

If every priest in the world tomorrow could be married and only one priest/religious choose celibacy, would this one priest's sacrifice be any less in the eyes of God, because his brother priests choose wedlock over celibacy? Do unfaithful wives and husbands influence God's view over faithful wives and husbands?

What is weakened is not celibacy itself, rather the public perception of celibacy, the credibility, behind which, the veiled celibate curtains of the Latin rite Catholic Church hide the children of the ordained.

What do you protect then, the tradition of celibacy, a vulnerable, respectable tradition when lived authentically or God's creation, a human being?

Do you veil the creator's creation so that you, as a priest or religious, mighty credibly appear as if you are honouring both creator and creation or do you honour the creation truthfully and authentically in the eyes of God?

Do you weaken their state, the mother and child, a fearful father, or do you strengthen their circumstance?

> "... you open a breach, a wound in the mystery of the Church."

The deeper wound is a wound that is caused by "lamentable defection", priests and religious having sex.

"Lamentable defection" is a Church and institutional wound and regrettable phrase, that penetrates to the very heart of the children of the ordained, psychologically, and historically.

Any physician (divine or otherwise) would treat the deeper wound that impacts children first, not the superficial wounds that involve adult-centered traditions.

Regarding the children of priests and religious, the "wound" of clerical sexual indiscretion is stitched up first, embarrassment hid, burying the reality of a much deeper wound, further inflamed by concealment.

This inflamed, concealed wound is hidden behind closed lips of children of priests and religious, sellotaped with institutional secrecy, *Silentium*.

This wound is psychological and is a menace, destroying children as it has done for centuries and will continue to unless it is recognised, addressed appropriately and for once children of the ordained put before clericalist and selfish ideals.

Viri Probati and *Parēns* can heal this wound for children moving forward, since both diminish *Silentium*

If celibacy is to continue, which it likely will, it must be humble.

Chaste celibacy is only as sacrificial as it is humble, and there is nothing modest about pretence. The tradition of chaste celibacy, if it remains, must be as humble as the cross it claims to be, humanly speaking, offering itself up, not the welfare of the children conceived, subsequently hidden in a mischievous attempt to preserve an image.

The tradition of celibacy should not obscure the reality that priests and religious will be parents, whether it is liked or not?

Moreover, how can something be considered sacrificial if it is not humble?

There is nothing modest about *Silentium*, it is not of God nor is it of consecrated chaste celibacy.

It is purely of human necessity to maintain the status quo regardless of detrimental consequences.

This is a bind that *Parēns* and *Viri Probati* can untie, consequently upholding the authentic sacrificial nature of chaste celibacy alongside children's natural rights within a marriage, simultaneously. The dignity of celibacy and the dignity of children of the ordained presume one another not the opposite.

The fallout thus, of the collective inability of the priestly and religious body globally to be absolutely and wholly celibate and chaste is a humble recognition on behalf of the institutional Catholic Church, that this procreative, collective inability must be discerned in advance by seminarians, with recourse to *Viri Probati*. The sidestep to this, by some, is the statement that celibacy is individual. However, celibacy is only as individual as it is not mandatory.

The failure of the Catholic priesthood to be always and wholly celibate and chaste should not negatively befall the offspring of priests and religious that will inevitably result. This is both unfair and anti-Catholic.

> "Priests [...] [need to] dedicate themselves to the upbringing of that child and taking care of the mother."
>
> (Cardinal Sean O'Malley, 2017)

I could not agree more, but why won't the Church, globally, allow a man to do that while working as a priest/religious? Why allow one rite and not another?

The Vatican has said this is not impossible, so if it is not impossible, would a wedding ring create pastoral difficulty, it does not posit problems for the Maronites and others? Is it because it has been accepted socially that this is not the norm, when, behind closed doors, priests and religious have become parents for centuries?

Pope John XI (Pontificate ended 936) was purportedly the son of Pope Sergius III, and Pope Silverius (Pontificate ended 537), son of Pope Hormisdas.

"In 1980, the Holy See, in response to requests from clergymen and laity of the Episcopal Church of the United States who were seeking full communion with the Roman Catholic Church, created a Pastoral Provision to provide them with special pastoral solicitude. [...] The ordination of married former protestant clergy began under Pope Pius XII. The Pastoral Provision gave a structure for the integration, formation and eventual ordination as Catholic priests who are married former Anglican Clergy. Under the Pastoral Provision, the ordination of married former Episcopal clergymen was made possible. [...] Since 1983 over 100 men have been ordained for priestly ministry in Catholic dioceses of the United States[.][...] In order to give due regard to the value of clerical celibacy, it is ordinarily the practice of the Congregation for the Doctrine of the Faith that the number of married priests in any particular diocese under the Pastoral Provision be limited to two." (Most Rev. Kevin W. Vann J.D.C., D.D)

I am confident that the hearts of these 100 Catholic priests in the USA are not divided between two types of fruitfulness. This

Pastoral Provision is the doorway through which, men who wish to become Catholic priests, discern their calling to the Catholic priesthood, men who have families.

Yet, their families are not considered an impediment to ministry; neither are children of priests considered an obstacle for Maronites.

The limitation of two admits to giving "due regard to the value of clerical celibacy."

However, the Pastoral Provision could act as a valuable tool to pragmatically implement *Viri Probati* as a response to the inevitability of children of clergy and religious, who deserve families not secrecy.

The existence of the Pastoral Provision moreover proves priests can and do act as priests and parents simultaneously. The unwillingness to do this on a larger scale is unfair. It must be noted that the Pastoral Provision grievously undermines the Impracticality Argument, regardless of however limited the scale of men permitted via the Pastoral Provision, may be.

One could write endless theological arguments surrounding this issue on either side of the divide and gain no ground.

Drafts of this book lie strewn across my desktop and office floor beneath my dog's chin as he looks up in complete wonderment. "What was wrong with this", I feel he muses as his beautiful eyes stare at me in a blend of love and tiredness, whilst privately, he deliberates, 'can we go for a walk now, it's been ages, I want to play.'"

These moments take me away from the self-absorbed world of the written and theological world and perhaps that's part of the problem, being too absorbed?

Adults become so absorbed by their world and belief system that they forget children. People will argue against this, will criticise *Parēns*, calling *Viri Probati* an abomination, weakening the law of celibacy, amid a flurry of complaints, like white sealed envelopes in sacks only to be poured out on the floor of the Catholic Church and my office, wishing for nothing to change. However, like myself, absorbed in my book, as my dogs daydream about trees, bushes, shrubbery and birds and nature, I am distracted.

We too as adults have become so distracted by our own desires, we see nothing only, what we want to see.

Reluctance to elicit change is a belief that the status quo is adequate.

However, the status quo is supported by non-acknowledgement, and behind this bricked wall of non-acknowledgement, are mute children. This needs to stop, since *Silentium* equates a pastoral and psychological genocide in the minds of the children of the ordained.

I would like to seat those for and against celibacy in a room. I would ask them one single question.

> "How do you propose the Catholic Church will care for the inevitable children of priests and religious of the future, avoiding baseless sentiment, fostering circumstances that support families of the ordained?"

It should soon become apparent that one can care for a child outside wedlock, even if within wedlock is the most preferred option.

With celibacy put away, we see, it is rightfully, only within an open relationship with one's child, one that is loving, where the needs of a child may openly be met, thus, *Parēns*.

The long-term answer means the implementation of *Viri Probati* also. Just as the children of the ordained are inevitable, the inescapable and accompanying reality that said children deserve a family not laden with poverty is undeniable, thus *Viri Probati*. In this, celibacy remains, is sanctified, and the children of the ordained are no longer marginalised.

> "This issue [*Viri Probati*] will probably be made the subject matter of a more detailed study of the issue with a view to the Church taking a consistent position, not only in view of the Amazon but in view of the universal Church."
>
> (Cardinal Peter Turkson., 2019)

A consistent position is indeed required.

However, this consistent position needs to be in harmony with child safeguarding, creating a safe and hospitable place for children. Is the price of implementing *Viri Probati* too high?

> "When speaking of children who come into the world, no sacrifice made by adults will be considered too costly or too great, if it means the child never has to feel that he or she is a mistake, or worthless or abandoned to the four winds and the arrogance of man." (Pope Francis, 2016)

If this statement is true, then the Catholic Church will immediately and without hesitation, stop all systemic processes that enable *Silentium*, and implement *Viri Probati*, as *Viri Probati* will dissolve the need for *Silentium*.

The Church will recognise that celibacy is in part, lived authentically and inauthentically, simultaneously, owing to human nature.

In other words, celibacy is intrinsically "fluid."

Consequently, punishment should not be the response to adult-centered incompetence (intermittent failure to be chaste and celibate) never befalling the children of the ordained domestically.

The children of the ordained of the future should be allowed to grow up without secrecy put upon them, a sinister secret that supports adult-centered needs, which is unfair and abusive.

It must stop. There is no good reason for it not to stop.

Implementing *Viri Probati* would be an effective treatment of the wound of "lamentable defection", or "procreative 'lamentable defection.'"

No good child-centred reason exists, that disallows implementation of *Viri Probati* (buoyed by *Parēns*).

However, by contrast, one good child-centered reason exists, these children deserve the light of the conjoined love of the eyes of their mother and father, not theological rebuttals that suggest celibacy is a greater sacrifice than the sacrifice these children bear secretly, within the eyes of an already omnipotent and omniscient creator, so celibacy appears absolute and unchallenged. This is undignified toward child and God.

> Yousef said, "my wife and children [...] are my everyday school of what it means to be a priestly father in the Church."

These words should remain in our hearts.

It is time to walk my dogs now.

It is time to drop my pen and wash my stained coffee cup, dark from the black hours and years of endlessly circumnavigating this issue.

It is time for dogs on a lead with butterflies and sun radiating off crystallised petals, and their metallic collars, reflecting damp hedgerow, as a suspiciously moist, Irish wind, cools my face amid the invisible, dwindling heat.

It is time for nature, never disguised, always honest and always promoting growth, as God intended it to be.

Though what walks with me, like ghosts, are an endless stream of children, the children of the ordained and religious.

They stare at me, with my head fallen, in my mind's eye, these thousands of children of the ordained, past, present and future.

I stare at the porous Irish stone upon which many mother's worried tears and father's anxious footsteps fell, in complete silence, over centuries, known only to God.

How many children lived and died in complete silence, in agony?

Was *Silentium* purgatory for these countless hidden children?

My heel drags across the rock, wherein I lay my prayer for them.

Then, barks fade in the distance as if to distract and comfort me with their childish play amid nature, as they dance in the moist fields around me, where tears hide and raindrops slide, lost within this foggy morning.

Chapter Six.

Using Coping International.

This book is concerned with proposing initiatives that combat abuse. This requires rationality, which requires absolute balance. The following words were expressed during the 2019 abuse summit at the Vatican during a press conference.

> "We do hope that one day we will get there; and that we will be the same amount as male religious present." (Sr. Carmen Sammut., 2019)

The words of Sr. Carmen Sammut, a woman I met with concerning the matter of children of priests and religious, former president of the UISG, the union of female religious globally, our meeting was fruitful and harmonious. I have great respect for her. Coping has examined the abuse of female religious in part. The only way to combat it is to empower women. To not enable God's creation is to disempower it and thus counteract creation. Am I calling for women's ordination? No, I am talking about hearing the voice of women at the ear of the Pope, the sound of truth, echoing throughout the Vatican, balanced with the already present and no less valuable view of men.

Clerical abuse cannot be combatted without hearing the voice of the woman, in equal measure as that of the male, at the Vatican. There must be an equal balance of humanity in Rome, male and female, influencing the sail of the ark, lest we, the Church, go in circles forever.

I do not condone nor wish to appear as licencing and legislating clerical, religious infidelity. If you are unfaithful to your celibacy and chastity vow or promise, or if you are unfaithful to your partner and have a relationship with a Catholic priest or religious, this is wrong, both on behalf of priest and woman concerned assuming a consensual relationship minus power imbalance. There is no getting past this immorality. Society can blame the Catholic Church for a lot of things, but individual decisions made by a man and a woman are just that, personal decisions.

No bishop or provincial made you do this. They specifically ask you not to do this. This act is made especially burdensome since the man is a priest or religious and the institutional scandal and fallout from uncovering the clerical sexual relationships differ if he was not a priest.

As the Catholic Church exists today, given that celibacy still exists and all priests and religious are called to be chaste, as are all Catholics, it is misguided to have a sexual relationship with a celibate priest or religious.

Fr. D. Vincent Twomey SVD notes.

> "Every sin, including sexual sins, are sins against justice. Adultery is an act of multiple injustices: against the child who may be conceived, against the injured spouse, and against God. The injustice against the child is based on the fact that the boy or girl would thus, generally speaking, be deprived of the normal (or optimal) conditions needed to mature, namely, a father and mother united in their parenting. This injustice is compounded if the father has taken a vow of celibacy and has caused a breach of sacred trust. In addition, there is the injustice in some cases of the

child being deprived of knowledge of his or her father's identity. The father of the child may be still ministering as a priest and be known to the child, enjoying the child's trust. When the true identity of the father eventually becomes known, the resultant experience of deception, confusion re one's identity, and breach of sacred trust can be traumatic." (Twomey., 2020)

Reflecting on Dr Twomey's considerations on the injustice suffered by the child, we note the child, not the circumstance should be of primary concern. The purpose of this book is to take the light off the adults and shine it peacefully upon the child conceived. Consequently, the Archbishop of Dublin notes.

> "Women who are mothers of the children of priests should not be ostracized or made feel shame of any kind. They are mothers and human beings before all else, and this ought to be respected regardless of circumstance." (Archbishop Diarmuid Martin., 2017)

Dr Twomey and Archbishop Martin's consensus are aligned in that "regardless of circumstance", "the injustice against the child" should be considered, "before all else." Too often, the circumstance is placed ahead of the child. This is a distraction technique which feeds *Silentium* and the Moral Argument.

Is highlighting the act, as a Catholic sin, judgemental? Is this a judgement in and of itself upon the mother painting her as scandalous? No, the purpose of highlighting this matter is not to judge, but to make people realise, *yes,* according to Catholic teaching, this is sinful, but that sinfulness is not what is primary. What matters now is, a child exists, and the child is what comes first, not our disillusion at the presence of alleged sinfulness. Let the adults discern their behaviour after we determine what the child's pragmatic and emotional needs are, which should come first. So do not judge the mother or father, help them help their child.

If this issue is to be remedied, only absolute truth will facilitate the situation being fixed, not avoidance, or shifting blame elsewhere.

By naming what is obvious, we can thus recognise that stating this over and over merely serves the interest of ignoring the child concerned. Two wrongs do not make a right.

The response of the Roman Catholic Church to this issue cannot be one that is unethical or indeed immoral. Nor can the answer be disguised as a moral, upright act unless it is intrinsically ethical. The Moral Argument cannot be viewed as a morally righteous sentiment in light of what some refer to as a Catholic sin, since promoting unemployment without good reason is uncalled for, and the birth of a child is not a just reason to make someone unemployed.

Hence *Parēns* and *Viri Probati* as an obvious solution as the Catholic Church looks forward.

The research for Coping International began in early 2012 when I first started approaching the Catholic Church.

However, in another way, the study started on the 19th of May 2011, the day I found out about my father.

Almost immediately, upon hearing the news, I felt deprived, deprived of an opportunity to tell my story. Everyone has a story, imagine depriving someone of that choice, and right?

I finally recognised that the absence of knowledge constitutes the presence of something, uncertainty, within my subconsciousness. I felt there was a truth surrounding me that was known but was intentionally being held back from me. Why? I did not know or understand. My material needs were always met in abundance, but interiorly I felt a dark vacuum which just expanded over time. Within that vacuum, was substance, hidden beneath years of layers of deceit, hiddenness and sadness. That sadness sought its reciprocity; thus, my grief became a seed.

I yearned for internal peace, thus *votum*, the *votum ecclesiae*, the words advised by my mentor many years ago in Maynooth.

For years I could not communicate or explain this to anyone.

How could I when I did not consciously know what was causing this silent grief and anxiety?

The light of certainty decayed in an ardent fog of denial regarding my identity. All of this, knowing and not knowing, promoted the formation of an idea.

Coping came about quite by accident.

I naïvely began speaking to people about my father, about having been quite suspicious throughout my childhood and having identified closely with Catholicism as a young man in a growingly secularised Ireland, which was unusual to some.

It was not until I told a small number of people about JJ being my father that people started to advise me to be silent. It was then that I decided against silence definitively.

I saw a profound resistance toward making visible, something that up to that point, was mostly unrecognisable as a social issue owing to the problem of accompanying non-acknowledgement, which my storytelling was unwittingly challenging. I might add, those who silenced me do not wear a collar, nor for the most part, are even practising Catholics.

Coping, Children of Priests International was born.

I believe God wanted it. I think the Holy Spirit inspired it. I pray that God stays near Coping to help it grow; otherwise, it is finished.

Out of the manure of imposed silence, I saw a seedling of an idea sprout and poke its nose above the arid soil of silence.

Coping was fed with rhetorical questions that surrounded the natural rights of children to elicit on the record responses from those who mattered.

However, this growth required help.

I naively turned to the Irish Government.

The government in the years before the Boston Globe's 2017 pioneering article, denied help repeatedly.

Among those who refused help was the then sitting Minister for Disability, Equality, mental Health & Older People.

The department wrote to me denying assistance.

> "Unfortunately[,] again I have to emphasise that [the] Minister cannot offer you any letter of support at this time." (Department of Health & Children, 2014)

I also asked the Minister for Children to provide a letter of support. Concerning this letter, the Archbishop of Dublin commented on the alleged letter via an email to me, dated January 2015.

> "[I] have no idea whatsoever about any such letter."

> (Archbishop Diarmuid Martin., 2015)

The Archbishop had received other letters of support from other sources at this time.

Interestingly, the Department of Children and Youth Affairs later stated in a letter send to me -referencing the alleged letter of support issued by the Department, following my request for a copy of the said letter, -

"it has not been possible to locate a copy of this correspondence."

(Department of Children & Youth Affairs, 2015)

This is just two denials. I printed off each email and letter received from the Government; they paint a picture of a systemic denial for assistance, more than two denials. However, was it the Government's place to help?

In 2016, the United Nations Concluding observations on the combined third and fourth periodic reports of Ireland called for,

> "measures to assist children fathered by Catholic priests in upholding their right to know and be cared for by their fathers, as appropriate, and ensure that they receive the necessary psychological treatment." (Committee on the Rights of the Child., 2016)

The Irish Government relentlessly and at every hurdle refused to help in any way during the formation of Coping.

The government deliberately and repeatedly refused to help, giving no reason, their mental health minister refused, and the department for children couldn't find the letter they allegedly sent in support of Coping, a letter the Archbishop confirmed he knew nothing of.

The Irish Government remained steadfast in not supporting this human rights issue.

I felt deeply hurt that the Irish State denied support toward children of priests and religious without reasonable cause, particularly in light of the UN 2016 recommendations regarding the children of the ordained and religious.

Why not offer a word of encouragement? Successive Irish promoted equality for all yet did not see the need to support children of priests and support their right to equality, despite my repeated efforts. Suffice to say, the wagons were circled, and I got no help, and neither did the children of priests.

One formal letter of encouragement could have annihilated non-acknowledgement that surrounds this issue.

Thank God the Church did help. Otherwise, I am not sure what I would have done. I was wrong to approach the Irish Government for assistance with a human rights issue; it seems to me that their approach to equality is equality for all except the children of the ordained

I thought I would have needed the Government's help.

That is why I approached them.

I was wrong and misguided in this assumption. However, this in no way excuses withholding support of a human rights initiative that was not requesting money. What possible reason could they have not to help, all we wanted was a word of encouragement?

In this regard, the Irish Catholic Church has absolutely outshined 1the State in the provision of encouragement of care and safeguarding toward vulnerable persons.

However, one man outside the Church, active in the Irish State, did the right thing, a man I have huge admiration for, the President of Ireland, Michael D. Higgins. He stood behind this effort inviting my fiancée and me to *Áras an Uachtaráin*, the Irish presidential house in Dublin, where we discussed the matter at hand.

President Higgins had a definite interest in the matter which may be linked in with the fact that he was a lecturer in political science and sociology during his impressive career.

I remain grateful to him for his support.

President Higgins is "supportive of the aims of Coping with regard to advancing the position and the rights of children." (President Michael D. Higgins. President of the Republic of Ireland., 2015)

To have a sitting President support Coping was and remains to be, immensely encouraging.

Coping was beginning to gain traction.

I thankfully had no problem whatsoever in Ireland, and the Irish Bishops deserve every credit in addition to AMRI Association of Leaders of Missionaries and Religious of Ireland, who supported and had faith in Coping since its genesis.

Many priests and religious in the background, who wish to remain anonymous, helped and continue to assist Coping.

I examined other scandals in the Catholic Church, from adoption to the sex abuse crisis and one common thread seemed apparent, accompanying poor mental health.

Thus, it made sense to promote positive mental health concerning this phenomenon so that those affected by it, might first engage with a therapist before pursuing it further so that they could make their needs known, in a healthy way.

Thus, the main object of Coping, now a registered charity is as follows:

> "Coping International facilitates free psychological and pastoral support for children of priests and religious, children of the ordained and religious. Coping advocates for the rights of children of priests with the institutional Catholic Church."

That is our guiding principle, facilitation of free psychological and pastoral support and advocacy.

It is a dual interdependent main objective.

Coping assists priests also who are struggling to come to terms with their situation, always toward the betterment of the child, helping the priest realise the best position for him to improve his child's chances.

It is imperative for him to remain happy and content. This is especially important, for parent and child.

I had heard from some people across the world through mutual friends and acquaintances, who are children of priests and religious before Coping was formally set up.

Many were from Africa, but Poland, parts of Asia, Australia, and America, north and south were the first countries I heard from, all children who had met the Catholic Church.

They all shared one collective experience; the Church dissuaded all from pursuing their story any further.

Some were threatened (albeit indirectly), some were manipulated, at which point they were given an "audience" with the Bishop or appointed individual, usually an hour. They told their story and then left; there was no structure to the meeting.

Whilst they recognised that they wanted to be heard, they did not identify what they needed. Some clergy, conscious of a desire to defeat the matter, when contacted a second time, would cleverly respond, stating the obvious.

> "I have listened to you and heard your story, owing to a hectic schedule at this time of year, I am not in a position to follow up at the moment. Be assured of my prayers for your intentions..."

The commonality of this type of approach said one thing, across a divide of cultures and contexts, dissuade, avoid, and bury.

The discouraged children of priests and their mothers were at a loss as to what to do? How could they be listened to, especially in cultures where Catholicism is a part of one's cultural identity?

I recognised that if these people were prepared and had adequate information relating to psychology, theology, and pastoral statements from episcopal conferences around the world, and the Vatican, then the mother or child would be better informed.

Thus, the tactic of dissuading, avoid, and bury would itself be entombed beneath natural rights seeking acknowledgement.

The first step was to identify how silencing as a central character to this could be recognised, officially as harmful.

What would formally come into law in Ireland in 2018, under the 2018 Irish Domestic Violence act, realised controlling, or coercive behaviour as criminal behaviour.

> "A person commits an offence where he or she knowingly and persistently engages in behaviour that— (a) is controlling or coercive, (b) has a serious effect on a relevant person, and (c) a reasonable person would consider likely to have a serious effect on a relevant person. (2) [...] [A] person's behaviour has a serious effect

on a relevant person if the behaviour causes the relevant person— (a) to fear that violence will be used against him or her, or (b) serious alarm or distress that has a substantial adverse impact on his or her usual day-to-day activities." (Domestic Violence Act., 2018)

"Adverse impact on his or her usual day-to-day activities", at the centre of this "adverse impact, were and still are, confidentiality agreements ransoming the needs of children of the ordained and religious against the deviant need for secrecy on behalf of individual clergy who promote *Silentium*.

Remember, confidentiality agreements are not always in the form of a legally binding contract but may be verbal or even assumed.

Child maltreatment, emotional abuse, and definitions of abuse as defined by the World Health Organisation, all describe in part, the experiences of children of priests and religious who suffer extreme psychological and emotional damage.

Building on the definitions, psychiatrists, Professor Patricia Casey, and Dr Helen Keeley both examined the issue of children of priests and religious in what was possibly one of the first publicly disseminated, via Coping, conclusions by a psychiatrist on the matter of the children of the ordained and religious and associated harms.

Information for the website was accumulating.

Over time, the Holy See would begin to examine this issue, and it was quickly evident for all to see, that actual teachings were naturally applicable to this phenomenon from a pro-life perspective.

Vatican departments including, the Dicastery for Laity, Family and Life, the Pontifical Commission for Safeguarding of Minors, the Discipline Section of the Congregation for the Doctrine of Faith, headed by Irishman, Monsignor John Kennedy, the Nunciature to the United Nations based in Geneva alongside the Congregation for Consecrated Life and the Congregation for Clergy, not to mention the newly formed Papal task Force, all engaged with Coping over time, each acknowledging the issue of children of priests and contributing to the development of knowledge and solutions to presenting problems.

Each one is located on Coping, and this ecclesial acknowledgement would go a long way to destabilising the longstanding force of non-acknowledgement so present within the minds of the children of the ordained and religious.

My idea was that children of priests and religious globally could go to the website following our press release and navigate with ease learning about this issue.

The site was designed primarily to bring one from page to page, starting with mental health-related information, statements by the Vatican and after that the Vatican Guidelines for the children of the ordained. The point is to educate and give substance to a largely invisible problem, children of the ordained and religious suffering.

An open letter from the Archbishop of Dublin, Archbishop Diarmuid Martin, follows the guidelines.

> "This letter is a greeting to you if you are the child of a priest, or if you are a woman who has had a child with a priest or indeed if you are a priest who has fathered a child and for whatever reason live in silence. I want you to know that there is a place for you in the Church; there exists pastoral support to assist your concerns." (Archbishop Diarmuid Martin., 2017)

Letters such as the beautiful letter penned by Archbishop Martin, sentiments and expressions of interest and confirmations of teachings and practises, both internal and external, alongside a moral treatise on the issue by Fr D Vincent Twomey SVD, are there to guide and educate, so that hour with the Diocesan or Religious Order prelate may be maximised in terms of its effectiveness.

Before mothers, priests, and children ever meet a diocesan representative, many come to Coping, and it is I who walk with them. I try my best to separate what they want from what they need.

A need is necessary; a want could be a fruit of negative emotion, thus psychology and counselling.

Walking with these people from around the globe is tiring, but inspiring and worthwhile. An enormous amount of trust is placed in me by exceedingly vulnerable persons, thus Coping works with a supervisor and other professionals to assist us.

Sometimes the person is nervous about approaching the Catholic Church institution about their situation, that is why I find it mesmerising when some Church authorities make statements that openly minimise the degree of clerical infidelity involving priests and religious who break their chastity and celibacy vow. Nobody knows except God, one can speculate, one can estimate, but chastity is privately lived. When it is broken by a priest or religious, owing to their profession, unchasteness is doubly private.

As the child of the ordained, mother or priest continues their journey through Coping's site, they will read many statements from episcopal conferences worldwide, alongside comments from the USG and UISG, unions of religious orders, male and female respectively, globally.

All comments are a recognition of the importance of this issue, thus enabling the person presenting to feel increasingly confident, that this is an issue of concern for Catholics across the world, from Rome to the Gambia and Sierra Leone, Canada, the Philippines and many more.

These statements exist to convey hope against a backdrop of expectant silence regarding this issue, for the person who is afraid.

The journey of discovery of all of this relevant information exceptionally crafted and researched by experts in their field from around the world is juxtaposed with a pastoral or psychological journey of discovery. The person is accompanied if they wish to be, whereupon they can offload their story in complete confidence. They are made to feel welcome and assured that they are absolutely and unequivocally, not alone, nor judged.

As they grow in confidence, their needs are identified.

We discern if we can establish links between their experience as the silenced child of a priest/religious with arising needs.

In other words, did secrecy or poverty that resulted, perhaps marginalisation or social isolation or exclusion generate inhospitable circumstances for the mother or child?

Did their conditions inhibit progress in terms of housing, schooling, or education? How did this affect their psychological development and overall, holistic promotion of human growth, physically, spiritually, and emotionally?

This reflective process is enabled and buoyed by the academic treatises made available freely on the site, where the child may lean their experiences on pertinent, contextually correct, information.

Thus, as they grow in self-awareness, equipped with relevant information their confidence grows, both in terms of conviction of their own ability to speak with the Catholic Church but also, in terms of being able to identify their needs, and how those needs developed in relation to their own circumstances.

There is a final section for priests because these men also deserve to be able to benefit from the information that is specific to them. All priest related materials rest on one assumption; transparency surrounding the child must be guaranteed in all circumstances. That child must be enabled and encouraged to be as transparent as they wish to be concerning their identity.

Canon law, specifically Cann. 384 is referenced on Coping for priests.

I queried this canon with a late, great Canon lawyer and expert in his field, Rev. Robert Kaslyn, SJ. I asked Rev. Kaslyn,

> "If a priest breaks his vow of celibacy and neglects a child, in such an instance would Canon 384 mean the

bishop/superior has a canonical onus to respond or does he share the responsibility to put the situation right?"

The late Rev. Kaslyn, a member of the faculty of the School of Canon Law, the Catholic University of America since 2001, confirmed the following.

"Since 1983, canon 384 would require that the bishop respond pastorally both to the priest who violated celibacy and to the woman involved. The priest has violated an essential obligation of his priestly life. (There was no direct connection between this canon in the 1983 code and a canon in the 1917 code). What the bishop does, exactly depends on circumstances of time and place: does the woman want him involved at all in the raising of the child? To what extent was there a relationship between the two people rather than a one-night visit? The answers would assist the bishop in determining how to act; he would want to make sure that the woman and child were taken of.[...]"

(Rev. Robert Kaslyn SJ., 2018)

The late Rev. Kaslyn's comments highlight the nature of the Catholic Church as a compassionate entity, and when the institution strays from that landmark, they are utterly lost at sea. However, if they adhere to precepts, noted by the late canon law expert, 'Kaslyn's lamp' will surely guide all to a shoreline of truth and transparency.

On more than on occasion, people have asked me to set up a branch of Coping in their own country. People's desire to help, to be a part of something is admirable and well-intentioned.

People have lamented that there exists no such initiative in their own respective country, giving this issue visibility.

Giving something visibility, a poster, a building, a placard, a megaphone, a face in every country, builds one thing only an organisation.

It sets up this organisation as petitioning the Catholic Church.

It designates this company as a lobby group, where the intention is to convince, or make something happen, peacefully or otherwise.

Coping exists to inform you to help you understand logically and teach you how to challenge the socially engrained behaviour *Silentium* precipitates.

So, what does one do? How do you spread the word?

The "battleground" of this clash, *Silentium* versus natural law, is not found in offices, local representatives, in the mouthpiece of a megaphone or multiple organisations.

Righteousness will be found in the courage of a mother, over coffee telling her friend, her priest, her family, her cousins, and neighbours, that this child is fathered by a priest or religious and that she needs help.

Righteousness is found in the clenched fist, armed with prayer and fever of each female religious who writes down the crimes inflicted upon them, emailing the Vatican, and including (cc) responsible and understanding media.

Involve everyone, then everyone has a duty of care to at least tell you if they can, how this issue can be solved?

Remember, you are not contacting journalists merely because you are the son or daughter of a priest; this would serve to undermine your dignity. However, the journalist's pen should always be at the ready if a social injustice exists within the Church, and you witness it.

If this injustice cannot be remedied or those responsible, clergy or laity, untiringly refuse to correct whatever injustice you have seen, then the journalist must be called. For if it festers in silence, it will hurt multitudes, and this is neither Catholic nor fair.

Righteousness is found in one individual standing up to tyrannical silence. Righteousness is not in bricks, mortar, placards, or shouting. However, you must begin with ridding yourself of any anxiety, emotional pain and that is done in counselling and openly chatting and letting go, discernible and slowly, of the imposed secret. Have a reliable care team around you. Then as you emotionally weaken and then strengthen, learn academically about the social, theological, and psychological responses available on Coping, freely for you.

Inform yourself, so you become your lawyer, judge, and jury.

You are not dependent upon anyone else.

Let your vulnerability and needs be your shield and let the world watch. No prelate, bishop, or concerned layperson can manipulate or silence you openly and call it Catholicism.

If your case is legitimate, they have a duty of care to care for you. If they do not, then go above them to the Vatican. If they beat you and surrender you to judgement and oppression, then this must be made known too, this is how the concept of vulnerability is a strength. Weakness should catalyse compassion, not further pressure.

If one mother owns the paternity of her child and refuses point blank to remain silent or indeed to impose the same silence upon her child(ren), then what if the next woman does the same, and the next and the next?

Truth must become the norm, not the exception, in these cases.

If you are a priest's child and an adult, and people still impose the condition of silence upon you, defy them. Especially in the case where your father is a priest and you as his child are an adult, remember what the Vatican has said of such scenarios.

> "In the situation where a priest who has 'children who are already grown up, 20- 30 years old […], in these situations, the Dicastery does not oblige the Bishop to invite the priests to request the dispensation' from priesthood owing to paternity. 'The Dicastery counsels a more flexible discernment within the rigorous practise and guidelines of the Congregation.'"

Not even the Vatican wants your silence.

In this situation, where a proverbial finger of fear is placed on your lips, pull back.

Put the truth in writing, email the respective Bishop/Provincial, cc' the Nuncio of your country and if you are brave enough, blind copy a journalist or two.

You may also cc' Coping if you wish.

If more know, more will expect justice.

A "let's keep this between us for now" mentality must be quashed, the second it is uttered, it is *Silentium* that must be buried, not people and their respective identities and right to freedom of speech. *Silentium* contradicts free will also, a central tenet of Catholicism.

If you are blessed with good shepherds as we are in Ireland, then all you will need is tea or coffee and a biscuit, I just wish it was as simple and straightforward everywhere, but unfortunately, it is not.

Sometimes you need the level of openness, that only a journalist can provide off the record initially, alongside the pressure the Congregation for Clergy or Congregation for Consecrated Life can place upon the diocese/order, respectively.

Choose wisely if you choose a journalist.

The words "off-record for now" are your motto you say over and over until you know what you want on the record.

Again, everything in writing, agreeing off the record, initially, with a view to putting that which you are comfortable with, on the record.

Sometimes, the Church and even your family need to know that you are taking back control of your own life and sometimes only an absolute stranger is your best ally.

Will there be fallout from your disclosure, yes!

However, ask yourself this, they made you live in a world decorated and adorned with secrecy and concealment, did family and Church ask if this would be ok by you?

No, they placed an emotional muzzle on you, neither allowing you to nurture yourself with what you needed nor allowing you to announce your cries. They made you live in this world.

Now a new world of transparency must emerge, where the real "brilliant jewel" is not a tradition but a child.

This does not mean the tradition is also not "brilliant", but it just highlights you as a human as being of primary importance.

So, if your father is a priest or religious, all you need is a highlighter and an email account.

Take excerpts from this book and highlight them alongside information freely available on Coping and when the tyranny of silence comes, allow it, and tell every one of those who silence you.

Then, they will be silent and not you. Then, if you can forgive, do, as hate is a heavy burden to carry.

In responding and meeting with the Catholic Church, make a list of your needs, discern how those needs emerged and if a loving, stable father was present, would those same needs have developed?

Start in the counselling room, announce your cries and wails there.

Then, reasoned, and more rational, less emotional, emerge, sensible, armed with the knowledge enabling you to talk to the Catholic Church provincial and bishop in their vernacular.

You do not need a lawyer, representative, attorney, or mediator.

If the bishop does not listen, then go above him:

1. Start with the Bishop/Provincial/Superior.

2. If Bishop/Provincial/Superior General (in the case of female religious), go above them to the President of the country's bishops or in the case of a religious, go to the national provincial or the superior general in Rome.

3. If they do not listen, go to the Congregation for Clergy / Congregation for Consecrated Life.

Always bring an off-record journalist with you (insofar as have spoken to one and be in touch with one) and tell the Church this.

Being off record does not mean you have to go public, but should you choose to, the journalist is aware of the story intimately.

This may take time, give them time.

Good journalism has the power to change the culture for the better. You can back out, and that is your prerogative, but you have the choice.

If the diocese/order/Vatican Congregation responds well, well in such a case, good for them and it is a good news story.

The journalist only types the story; you and the Catholic Church create it! Therefore, your vulnerability is your strength and is far more effective than any megaphone or placard.

Whilst it will not make you popular with some, always email, with the same by snail mail if requested when sending information to the Catholic Church.

If you are asked not to email, disregard, send maybe two (kind) emails a day until the silence breaks.

One can prove an email, you cannot prove a letter, even if it was registered.

All that a registered letter shows is that a message was sent, not what was said.

Always let yourself be guided by your needs, not your wants, that is the point of counselling, being open about the truth and talking, it allows you to discern need from want.

Consequently, what emotional, psychological, developmental (housing, education) needs have you?

How were you affected by this unwanted secrecy that you inherited at birth? What did it do to you, how did it condition you, what was expected of you?

Now compare that same experience against one of your friends who had no such conditioning and expectations placed upon them. Do you see a difference?

On earth, you are your lawyer, judge and jury, attorney, and mediator. You are all you need, so begin to speak up, stand for your rights, soon you will see the wolves in sheep's clothing emerge from the darkness they imposed upon you attempting to keep you quiet, those who foster *Silentium*, and then with one flash of a journalists camera, they are suddenly famous.

Such is their vulnerability, not yours. Speak! Those who wish you to be quiet, their argument dies the first moment you open your mouth. Therefore, your vulnerability is your strength, always.

Those who insist on what is called *Silentium* may fear-monger, try to dissuade you from telling the truth. They may bribe, attack, isolate, anything to keep you from telling the truth. Bear in mind, this behaviour often occurs on behalf of the family, and it is not always the Church who silence. However, the Church too, engage in practices that promote *Silentium*.

Consider, is that your purpose in life, to guard a secret so another can appear as uniform, obedient, sacrificial and another, a woman, would not feed embarrassment or shame?

Shame on them for doing to you, what has been done, silenced, manipulated, and neglected by a desire to conceal indiscretion.

People will most likely be angry at your transparency and disclosure of priestly paternity. However, this negativity is out in the open and can be discussed and dealt with, whereas the cancerous fruit of *Silentium* festers internally, corroding all that is good with a smile on the face of the child who is harmed.

To the mother, if you are caught between a rock and a hard place, if the priest/religious is saying to you, "tell, and I will lose my ability to provide for you and the child", know that the intensity of your suffering does not protect you nor your child, it manipulates your child.

Remember, whatever happens to you, has happened to your child also.

For making you hold up this secret, the Catholic Church owes you an apology, and whomever else insisted upon it, some of whom may be outside the Church, which may include family and friends. Sometimes family are supportive, which is always beneficial.

The Catholic Church must ensure you and the child are adequately cared for.

The Moral Argument is gravely insufficient.

Remember the words of the late Rev. Robert Kaslyn, whom we spoke of earlier in the book.

> "Since 1983, canon 384 would require that the bishop respond pastorally both to the priest who violated celibacy and to the woman involved. [...] [The Bishop] would want to make sure that the woman and child were taken of; [...] to ensure support and definitely fulfilling any obligations of fatherhood." (Rev. Robert Kaslyn SJ., 2018)

The Catholic Church cannot canonically or ethically send you, the father and child(ren) down the road, with nothing in your future other than fear.

If they do, contact Coping and a good journalist.

Do not ransom your child's psychological needs against his/her material needs, allowing only one to be fulfilled.

This is abuse, even if you believe it is the only way; there is always another way, remember this.

To the priest, yours is a burden that is indeed unique.

You chose a young man not to have a family, in good faith and with good intentions. Now, you have a family. You want to provide for them but feel if you open your mouth, the mouths of your children will remain unfed, so you feed them with secrecy and concealment, knowing you are harming them and yourself in the process.

You fear you are avoiding a greater danger, the danger of sensation and being targeted by media.

I say to you, go to your Bishop and/or provincial. Suppose you do not want to get married and are not living in concubinage and then tell the truth. The secret is already corroding whatever goodness God placed in your child, daily.

Read the Vatican Guidelines for the children of the ordained and religious available on Coping and speak in complete truth with your superior.

If you and the mother of your child do not wish to marry and you can recommit to celibacy and chastity, speak about *Parēns* to your superiors.

If they suspend you calling it a "period of discernment", ensure that there are options to discern and that the outcome of this discerning period is not a foregone conclusion.

This is in your child's interests.

Otherwise, if a Bishop/Provincial forces you out, they have fired you for being a parent. Call it concubinage, call it what you want. The basics are the same. A father now has no job because he is a parent, and a child cannot eat. Canon law should never overrule common sense. Indeed, as the Congregation for Clergy acknowledged, albeit indirectly, in August 2020, citing the "the subtle discernment required in each instance." (Congregation for Clergy., 2020)

Consider, has the diocese/order helped, in locating another job and suitable accommodation, putting you on a path where you can care for yourself, as clerical to lay transition is complicated in many ways? This transition occurs at the same time a child is growing up, thus making the situation increasingly complicated.

If you stay in ministry, do not dare deny your child, least your paternity and priesthood fail. Allow him or her to recognise you as their father openly so. Society will mend itself, a child may not. Remember this.

Work with your bishop/provincial and encourage openness and honesty. In the long run, it is the best option.

If you leave and you have no choice, this is an abusive act by those forcing your hand. Even if the church can condone it canonically. But what they favour canonically is not always commendable, ethically speaking. If this happens, make it public, even anonymously. This is a darkness that must be exposed.

Finally, ask yourself these questions if you have left the ministry. These questions apply all priests, and religious, male, and female: bishops and provincials would do well to let these simple inquiries guide them in discerning this issue when it presents itself.

1. Is your child(ren) happy, and can they tell the truth about your priesthood/religious life and having to leave?

2. Are you, the mother of your child and the child assured of your next meal?

3. Are you, the child and the child's mother assured of a safe and warm place to live?

4. Are you, the child, and the mother, happy and content? If not, why not?

Now reflect on your ministry, before you became a priest, or indeed a religious. If someone came to you, a parent, and told you their children were forced to lie about their unemployment status, what would you say?

If they confirmed that they consequently were not sure how their families would manage to get another meal, were facing possible homelessness, if they concluded that these situations existed because of an act occurred, that was allegedly for Christ's Church. What would you say?

> "I tell you the truth when you did it to one of the least of these my brothers and sisters, you were doing it to me!"
>
> Matthew 25:40.

And I turn to you again, the child and in doing so, I turn to your family and friends around you. You cannot claim to be Christian, Catholic or a proponent of equality if you deny what is natural to the children of the ordained and religious.

Allow your family the same natural freedoms that we all expect, even if it is uncomfortable. If it is painful, make it comfortable, do not make it harder than it already is. It is better that we as adults bear such pain or discomfort than a child interiorly and without knowledge or understanding or the ability to vocalise that which is happening to them.

Finally, I wish to address the child of the ordained/religious.

You are not a pillar that holds in place a structure that predates you. If you and many like you stand up and are counted and recognised, indeed a tradition may "weaken", recollecting Cardinal's Sarah's concern.

And what of it? A tradition can regenerate itself; you may not regenerate fully.

Besides, what should support celibacy is not you, but obedience, clerical disobedience, and disobedience is not your master.

Stand up and shake off the dust of history from your clothes weighted beneath years of neglect and be free.

If you live in a culture or context where the Bishop or Provincial is seen as a "big man in society," as one African grandmother recently lamented, having heard of her priest son's indiscretions and the child's subsequent desire for transparency, be the bigger person.

Know the code of faith that guides the Church, for ethically speaking, Catholicism is on your side, regardless of your faith beliefs.

In the context of the African grandmother above, the matriarch wished for silence, the child, for freedom.

The adult child broke the code of silence and went all the way to Rome.

Today, she is on a path of righteousness and peace.

Perhaps, had her father been a bigger man, then she would not be so upset and lost today, but she will get there, eventually, this I trust.

It was the African grandmother's conditioned perspective of the bishop, that led to her mounting fear that the "big man" would punish the family.

Let culture not dictate to you, let silence not dictate to you, let clerical disobedience not dictate to you, let neither mother nor father, nor bishop nor provincial, nor society nor police (in whatever form that may take) dictate to you.

Let only the God-given natural rights that you are endowed with by virtue of your humanity be your compass.

Change culture, do not be its bedfellow.

Inform society, do not listen to it when it whispers into your soul, behaviours that neglect a child. For if you obey those who foster *Silentium*, then you too become a manufacturer of that which intergenerationally harms children.

Do you wish to harm a child? No!

Then, be that child's example for freedom. It is time for a new world.

Recently, I asked a friend, a journalist about giving their email as an example of whom to contact to go on record having read this book. She replied, "knowing how many there are [children of priests], it is not something we could handle."

Borrowing my friend's reflection, if the world cannot handle you, us, then let society, tradition, and Church, all break together as one. That is eucharistic.

I would much rather be broken with you than break you.

It is better this way, rather than the unbroken standing upon the silence of the most vulnerable, a muted child, throughout history.

And so, that is why we, as children of priests and religious, do not need multiple organisations, placards, and gimmicks.

You only need courage, the courage to stand and to know you are not alone.

Now you know you are part of a global and historical group, rather than building up an organisation, build yourself up, interiorly.

Remember, you need the peace of mind that good mental health brings so you can understand the interior workings of the institution of the Catholic Church.

Then, with a sound mind, informed by Catholicism (as a believer or non-believer), you can take apart the menacing secrecy that is hundreds of years old, all on your own, highlighting Catholic hypocrisy at every turn!

That is the power and intention of Coping, to empower you and teach you so you can liberate yourself.

Learn, represent break free, disobey *Silentium*, do not remain silent and be imprisoned.

You are already free.

However, those who are nearest you may have convinced you otherwise since you were born that you are not allowed absolute freedom. Acknowledge this deception, its roots, intention and overcome it.

Now it is time for a glorious rebirth.

Remember, all you need is a clear head, reason, and courage and no prelate or layperson can talk you down. You do not need megaphones, placards, paint or rotten fruit to throw. You need to understand, that which the Catholic Church, clergy and lay, preach, can be refracted back at them, through the lens of the neglect you suffered.

Catholicism preaches about dignity, say this back to them, and do it in writing, keep records.

No lawyer can do this for you or as well as you, and you are well able to speak to the Catholic Church, you are, after all, the child of a priest!

To those who do not like the presence of journalists, alongside the suggestion of calling and involving them, to you, I say, do the right thing, then you can sleep peacefully.

Dear child, now go, lift the phone, ask for the private secretary of the Bishop or Provincial! Ask for the secretary's email address. Make sure it is not an administrative secretary, not to undermine their significant worth, but *generally* speaking, each provincial, superior general or bishop has a private secretary.

This is the person that you need.

Write down your truth, the whole truth and nothing but the truth and point out precepts of Catholicism that contradict the silence imposed upon you since birth, which is masked -wrongly so- as Catholicism. Be succinct and to the point, factual and appeal to common sense.

Whether you are a Catholic or not, write it all down in that email. Copy (cc) the Nuncio and Coping if you wish and maybe a journalist or two, write the words "off-record, for now."

If you are a woman and you are nervous about approaching the church, know that I have witnessed countless women approach the Church authorities regarding this phenomenon, worldwide, both mothers and daughters.

In each instance, they have shown themselves to be ferociously strong, fiercely determined and always that strength and determination were led with intelligence and not a placard anywhere to be seen. Use your head, use your mind, sons, daughters, mothers, and fathers, and you will do well, always.

Then, with the click of the button, 'send', the secret that buried you is decimated, annihilated and you are resurrected from the hell of imposed, unwanted and anti-Catholic silence, *Silentium*, that you as children were born within.

I thank you for reading *Our Fathers*, genuinely, thank you regardless of whether you agree with me or not, thank you.

Your contribution to this continued conversation hereafter is valued and always should be expressed in an approach that is conducive to child-centeredness, thus, politely and respectfully.

The most potent argument for the existence of married clergy is the existence of priests own, inevitable children, who according to Catholic tenets, are entitled to a mother and father and suitable means by which to provide for said children.

The inevitability of children of the ordained and religious ought to be informed by Catholic theology of marriage, not platitudes contingent upon the Moral Argument, that harm intergenerationally.

Thus, both *Parēns* and *Viri Probati* need wide acceptance and implementation, if the children of the ordained and religious and their parents and families are ever to be allowed to breathe freely, psychologically speaking.

If the Roman Catholic Church does not implement *Viri Probati* allowing those not called to be celibate and chaste, allowing expression of the innate desire to be parents within the context of the family as married clergy, they will indefinitely and psychologically detain the children of the ordained within the darkness of hiddenness and pain, *Silentium*.

Winter has come.

Cold frost lays upon the ground.

Frozen in the distance, fields and trees seem as if death has wholly embraced them.

However, spring will arrive.

Then, new blossoms will emerge, ripened in the ploughed earth of the past, relentlessly moiling and emerging from the dark earth of *Silentium* and all that goes with it.

For the innocence of the future depends upon the reality of the past being examined honestly in the present, and this is "the truth, and the truth will set [us] free." (John 8:32.)

Epilogue.

As I sit and write these words, one of my dogs sits and looks at me.

He is really beautiful and is a mixed breed. My other two dogs welcomed him without hesitation when he first arrived. His size, breed, playful nature, and insatiable hunger do not influence their welcome; the welcome is based only on the instinct of loving.

Why can't children of priests experience the same welcome inside and outside the church?

When did the instinct of hate penetrate the institution of the church to the point that they do not openly welcome people like me, like my brother and sister children of the ordained and religious globally?

When did it become constructive or facilitative toward evangelisation that one marginalises a priest for fathering a child, or slanders a woman who is pregnant, or abandons a religious sister into deplorable conditions, because of a child?

If you still believe in such actions having read this book, I encourage you to reread this book.

When did it become ok to condemn abortion but not to condemn the psychological annihilation of countless children in an effort to preserve institutional purity?

When did all of this become ok?

The transition of unacceptability to neutrality to acceptability was so gentle and subtle that it was barely observed, however, marginalising children nonetheless became the norm.

Then, unfortunately, it was considered catholic, and remains so, via the Moral Argument. Thus, you must contribute to the eternal demise of all that is condemnatory toward the children of the ordained and religious, *Silentium* and the Moral Argument

When a Cardinal or priest or Pope promotes unemployment as the first option for a new parent, something has taken a terrible turn for the worse, logic, sense and Catholicism have been replaced by greed and selfishness.

The catholic church needs married priests, not only because there is a shortage of priests, but because there is a shortage of good priests who are good fathers. Thus, the catholic church must enable, not disable, these priests and religious, assisting them in becoming good and responsible parents.

Those who wish to be celibate may commit to celibacy, but a commitment to a child regardless of one's marital status should always come before adult needs.

The dogs now play at my feed, tired waiting for me.

So too, the children of the ordained have grown weary of waiting on the institution of the catholic church to legislate improvements for their lives and the lives of the children of the ordained in the future.

Not legislating for married clergy (*Viri Probati*) in no way assists celibacy.

This inaction toward *Viri Probati* merely conceals the part inauthentic nature of celibacy hidden within the closed mouths of the children of the ordained, weakening it internally, spiritually, and theologically.

The inevitability of the children of the ordained of the future should anticipate the enabling of circumstances that are pragmatic as well as moral, circumstances that will help children of the ordained and their families.

What is the alternative?

We tell the children of the ordained of the future,

"yes we realised that not all moms and dads want to marry, we recognised the Moral Argument is gravely impractical and deceptive, alongside *Silentium*, but we still dismissed your parents without a clue as to how they may care for you. We did not facilitate or enable them positively and all of this, we promoted as being catholic, ethical and moral."

You could finish with "sorry" or write a cheque, but I do not think that would fix the situation for the child.

Promoting the dignity of a child is an undignified act *unless* the said promotion is accompanied by realism, practicality, openness, acceptance, pragmatism, and joy.

Valid promotion of child dignity actualises that which any dignified person knew already.

One does not just say something should happen; they enable and foster the right action, ensuring what is said is done. Even God recognises this, for Saint Joseph was a carpenter and provided for his child.

Though now, I will retire to my dogs for they have waited long enough, much like the children of the ordained, who await the company of kindness from those closest to them.

The night is approaching, though the dawn will arrive, when their bark of jubilant freedom will be heard by all those who wish to hear and even those who do not, and that too is ok.

Amen.

To Rome, they look with ardent glance,

to those whose cassocks upon cobbles dance.

Will the stroke of a pen upon documents grand,

allow father and child, together, to stand?

Key terms.

I. **_Silentium_**, the process of silencing the child of an ordained person or religious, concerning the child's identity as the child of an ordained person/religious, whilst forsaking the child's intrinsic right to freedom and choice.

II. **The Moral Argument**, the unceasing and unyielding claim that a priest or religious must leave priesthood, ministry, in every case, if he (or she in the case of a female religious) becomes a parent. The Moral Argument is a form of coercive control.

III. **_Parēns,_** refers to the situation where a Latin Rite priest who becomes a parent and latterly recommits to his priestly obligations in full (including chastity & commitment to celibacy), whilst simultaneously, openly acknowledges his biological child, as he continues to work as a celibate, chaste Roman Catholic Latin rite priest. The Holy See in January 2020 admitted, such a position is "not impossible." (Clergy., 2020)

Bibliography.

1. Achacoso, F. J. (2017, February 16). Sexual misconduct in the Philippines' Catholic Church: Sins of the Father | 101 East. (A. Jazeera, Interviewer) Retrieved from https://www.youtube.com/watch?v=CP6XU_Hymbo

2. Allen, E. A. (2020, July). *Crux*. Retrieved from CruxNow.: https://cruxnow.com/vatican/2020/07/vatican-official-laments-system-of-dominance-submission-for-women-religious/?utm_content=buffer0a5b2&utm_medium=social&utm_source=facebook.com&utm_campaign=buffer

3. al-Rahi, C. B. (2018, January). Via Email.

4. Andrea Tornielli. Vatican Director of the Dicastery for Communications. (2020., March 31). Hidden Children of

the Church. Retrieved from

https://www.bbc.co.uk/sounds/play/m000gtnw

5. Anglican Communion Director for Communications. (July , 2020.). *Via Email.*

6. Anglican Director for Communications. (2020., July). Via Email.

7. Archbishop Diarmuid Martin. (2015, January 15). Via Email.

8. Archbishop Diarmuid Martin. (2017). *Coping International.* Retrieved from http://www.copinginternational.com/wp-content/uploads/2017/03/OPEN-LETTER-FROM-THE-ARCHBISHOP-OF-DUBLIN.pdf

9. Archbishop Eamon Martin. (2019). *The Protection of Minors in the Church.* Maynooth: The Furrow.

10. Archbishop Paul-Nabil Sayah. (2020, October. 12). Via Email.

11. Ardura., F. B. (2020, June - August). Via Email.

12. Bennett., P. (2011). *Abnormal and Clinical Psychology. An Introductory textbook.* (Third. ed.). Bernshire.: Open University press.

13. Biggar, N. (2016, December 11). On the Principle of Double Effect. Retrieved from https://www.youtube.com/watch?v=E2Y_kidtlgQ

14. Bishop Robert C. Morlino. (2012, November 1). Open our eyes, Lord. *Diocese of Madison Catholic Herald.* Retrieved from http://www.madisoncatholicherald.org/bishopscolumns/3587-2012-11-01-morlino-column.html

15. Cardinal Blaise J. Cupich. (2019, March).

16. Cardinal Claudio Hummes. (2019, July).

17. Cardinal João Braz de Aviz. (2020, February). Bisogna cambiare. *Donne Chiesa Mondo.* Retrieved from https://media.vaticannews.va/media/osservatoreromano/pdf/donne/2020/02/Donne_febbraio_2020.pdf

18. Cardinal Jorge Bergoglio. . (2010). *On Heaven & Earth*. Random House Publications.

19. Cardinal Joseph Ratzinger. (2005, April 18). *Vatican.Va*. Retrieved from http://www.vatican.va/gpII/documents/homily-pro-eligendo-pontifice_20050418_en.html

20. Cardinal Manuel Clemente. (2019, May). Abusos Sexuais: Bispos comprometem-se a criar estruturas de «prevenção e acompanhamento» para proteção de menores. Retrieved from https://agencia.ecclesia.pt/portal/abusos-sexuais-bispos-comprometem-se-a-criar-estruturas-de-prevencao-e-acompanhamento-para-protecao-de-menores-em-atualizacao/

21. Cardinal Peter Turkson. (2019, October). *Catholic News Agency*.

22. Cardinal Robert Sarah. (2020, January. 25). Cardinal at center of 2 Popes storm doubles down on celibacy. Retrieved from

https://cruxnow.com/vatican/2020/01/cardinal-at-center-of-2-popes-storm-doubles-down-on-celibacy/

23. Cardinal Sean O'Malley. (2017, August). *http://cardinalseansblog.org/*. Retrieved from http://cardinalseansblog.org/2017/08/page/2/

24. Cardinal Stella. (2019). *Vatican News,*. Retrieved from https://www.vaticannews.va/en/vatican-city/news/2019-02/children-of-priest-cardinal-stella-interview-andrea-tornielli.html

25. Catholic Bishops Conference of England & Wales. (2018, July). *Coping International.* Retrieved from http://www.copinginternational.com/episcopalstatements/

26. Catholic Bishops Conference of Scotland Episcopal Secretary. (2014). Via Email.

27. Catholic Bishops Conference of Scotland. (2018). Via Email.

28. Catholic Professional Standards Ltd. . (2019). *Catholic Professional Standards Ltd.* . Retrieved from https://www.cpsltd.org.au/safe-church/national-catholic-safeguarding-standards/

29. Cholij, R. (n.d.). *www.vatican.va*. Retrieved from http://www.vatican.va/roman_curia/congregations/ccle rgy/documents/rc_con_cclergy_doc_01011993_chisto_en.html

30. Clergy., C. f. (2020, January). Addendum to Vatican Guidelines. Vatican City State. Retrieved from http://www.copinginternational.com/vaticanguidelines/

31. Committee on the Rights of the Child. (2016). *Concluding observations on the combined third and fourth periodic reports of Ireland.* Retrieved from http://docstore.ohchr.org/SelfServices/FilesHandler.ash x?enc=6QkG1d%2FPPRiCAqhKb7yhsvOufvUWRUJlLHi LHKqpXZxUGOtzQF0l%2B37QzAK0sbh7yc40d4J3IynFa Wf0Egu6J99RK6Y%2FTHjpged5r1H3f3KQIiFieFk0eAP ALAwKpbZz

32. Congregation for Clergy. (2020, July). Via Email.

33. Congregation for Clergy. (2020, August). Vatican.

34. Congregation for Clergy. (2020, january 20). Vatican City State. Retrieved from http://www.copinginternational.com/vaticanguidelines/ he-holy-see-agreed-that-such-a-situation-is-not-impossible-but-that-each-case-be-examined-on-its-own-merits-and-its-own-particular-circumstances/#prettyPhoto[postimages]/0

35. Congregation for Clergy. (2020, January). Via Email. Retrieved from http://www.copinginternational.com/wp-content/uploads/2020/01/Confirmation-of-Meeting-Statements-with-Holyv-See-2020..pdf

36. Congregation for Clergy. (2020, November 07). Via Email.

37. Congregation for Clergy. (2020.). Retrieved from Coping International.: http://www.copinginternational.com/vaticanguidelines/

38. Coping International. (2017, October.). Coping Press Release. Retrieved from http://www.copinginternational.com/wp-content/uploads/2017/02/Meeting-between-Coping-International-1.pdf

39. Coping International. (2020, January). Coping International. *Vatican Guidelines Approved Addendum.* Retrieved from http://www.copinginternational.com/vaticanguidelines/

40. DCYA. (2011.). Retrieved from www.dcya.gov.ie

41. DCYA. (2020). *Department of Children and Youth Affairs.* Retrieved from https://www.tusla.ie/services/child-protection-welfare/definitions-of-child-abuse/

42. Department of Children & Youth Affairs. (2015, March 23).

43. Department of Health & Children. (2014, May 7).

44. Diocese of Elphin. (n.d.). Celibacy.

45. Domestic Violence Act. (2018). Retrieved from http://www.irishstatutebook.ie/eli/2018/act/6/section/39/enacted/en/html

46. Donadio., R. (2009, October 21). Offer Raises Idea of Marriage for Catholic Priests. *The New York Times.* Retrieved from https://www.nytimes.com/2009/10/22/world/22church.html

47. Doyle., V. (2020, July). *Coping International.* Retrieved from http://www.copinginternational.com/terminology/

48. Dr Edward Simonton OGS. (2020, September 09). Via Email.

49. Father Oliver Treanor. (2020., September.). Private Communication used with permission. Father Oliver Treanor is a priest of the Diocese of Down and Connor, Ireland.

50. Ferrarotti, F. (2020, July). Via email.

51. Fr Jim Achacoso. (2020). Via email.

52. Francesca Starita, G. d. (2018, December 18). *Alexithymia and the Reduced Ability to Represent the Value of Aversively Motivated Actions*. Retrieved from https://www.frontiersin.org: https://www.frontiersin.org/articles/10.3389/fpsyg.2018.02587/full

53. French Episcopal Conference. (2019). *Coping International*. Retrieved from http://www.copinginternational.com/episcopalstatements/

54. Gledhill., R. (2019, April.). Vatican reveals more about guidelines on children of priests. *The Tablet*. Retrieved from https://www.thetablet.co.uk/news/11639/vatican-reveals-more-about-guidelines-on-children-of-priests

55. Gomes, J. F. (2019, May). Via Email.

56. Gracias., c. O. (2020, September. 12). Via Email.

57. Harrison, B. W. (n.d.). *Living Tradition.* . Retrieved from http://www.rtforum.org/lt/lt149.html

58. His Eminence Card. Joseph Ratzinger. (2005, April 18). CAPPELLA PAPALE MASS «PRO ELIGENDO ROMANO PONTIFICE» HOMILY OF HIS EMINENCE CARD. JOSEPH RATZINGER DEAN OF THE COLLEGE OF CARDINALS. Vatican City State. Retrieved from http://www.vatican.va/gpII/documents/homily-pro-eligendo-pontifice_20050418_en.html

59. International., C. (2020). *Coping.* Retrieved from http://www.copinginternational.com/vaticanguidelines/

60. Irish Catholic Bishops Conference. (2015., March). Retrieved from http://www.copinginternational.com/vaticanguidelines/

61. Irish Catholic Bishops Conference. (2017, August 17). *Catholicbishops.ie.* Retrieved from https://www.catholicbishops.ie/2017/08/31/principles-of-responsibility-regarding-priests-who-father-children-while-in-ministry/

62. Irish Catholic Bishops Conference. (2018, April). *Coping International.*

63. Irish Institute for Biosynthesis. (2020, August). *What is Biosynthesis?* Retrieved from http://www.biosynthesisireland.ie/about/what-is-biosynthesis/

64. Jazeera., A. (2017, February 16). Sexual misconduct in the Philippines' Catholic Church: Sins of the Father | 101 East. Retrieved from https://www.youtube.com/watch?v=CP6XU_Hymb0

65. John L. Allen Jr., P. S. (2001, March). Sister Marie McDonald in Reports of abuse Aids exacerbates sexual exploitation of nuns, reports allege. *http://natcath.org.* Retrieved from https://natcath.org/NCR_Online/archives2/2001a/0316 01/031601a.htm

66. Kahn, S. (2013, August 6). Effects of prenatal stress can affect children into adulthood. *TheConversation.Com.* Retrieved from https://theconversation.com/effects-of-prenatal-stress-can-affect-children-into-adulthood-16332

67. Kotze, F. V. (2020). Email.

68. Kotze., F. V. (1987.). *Stress among Roman Catholic Priests in South Africa.* Johannesburg., South Africa.: Wharton-Wheeler Library, Witwatersrand University (Wits) Johannesburg.

69. Lamb., C. (2020). Pope reveals why he said 'no' to married priests. *The Tablet.* Retrieved from https://www.thetablet.co.uk/news/13334/pope-reveals-why-he-said-no-to-married-priests?fbclid=IwAR31lL3v-BEidfsGPCRoA47tYYjqNIvT9G-5jAp7UUKOS0Y2wU7JosgGh6M

70. Louis J. Cameli. (2019, May 6). *America. The Jesuit Review.* Retrieved from americamagazine.org/faith/2019/05/06/hopes-and-challenges-priestly-celibacy-today

71. Maltese Episcopal Conference. (2018). *Coping International.* Retrieved from http://www.copinginternational.com/episcopalstatements/

72. Marie McDonald. (2020, July). Via Email.

73. Martin., A. D. (2015, January 15).

74. Martin., A. D. (2019, September 24). The Hidden Children of the Catholic Church | Foreign Correspondent. (L. Miller., Interviewer) Retrieved from https://www.youtube.com/watch?v=PADNmpeZEeM

75. Martin., A. D. (2020, November.). Dr. Diarmuid Martin, Archbishop of Dublin. Dublin. Retrieved from https://www.rte.ie/radio/radioplayer/html5/#/radio1/21858838

76. McGarry, P. (2019, April 22). Diarmuid Martin Q&A: If the Irish church wants to survive it has to change. *Irish Times*. Retrieved from https://www.irishtimes.com/news/social-affairs/religion-and-beliefs/diarmuid-martin-q-a-if-the-irish-church-wants-to-survive-it-has-to-change-1.3867406

77. McKeown., B. D. (2020, September. 2). *Catholic Bishops*. Retrieved from

https://www.catholicbishops.ie/2020/09/02/the-right-thing-is-rarely-the-easy-thing-bishop-donal-mckeown/

78. Most Rev. Kevin W. Vann J.D.C., D.D. (n.d.). Retrieved from http://www.pastoralprovision.org/

79. O'Reilly, P. (2020, May). Experiencing Stress in the Womb.

80. O'Sullivan, O. (2001.). Children Learn What They Live. *The Nationalist.*

81. O'Sullivan., O. (2011, December). Ireland's Identity. *Doctrine and Life.*, pp. 17-26.

82. Pope Francis. (2013, July 26). *Vatican.* Retrieved from http://www.vatican.va/content/francesco/en/speeches/2013/july/documents/papa-francesco_20130728_gmg-conferenza-stampa.html

83. Pope Francis. (2016). Amoris Laetitia.

84. Pope Francis. (2013, June 26). Retrieved from https://www.youtube.com/watch?v=5M2BDvveFXY

85. Pope Francis. (2013, June 26). Pope Francis: The spiritual fatherhood of priests. Vatican City. Retrieved from https://www.youtube.com/watch?v=5M2BDvveFXY

86. Pope Francis. (2019). Press Conference on the Return Flight from Abu Dhabi to Rome. Retrieved from http://www.vatican.va/content/francesco/en/speeches/2019/february/documents/papa-francesco_20190205_emiratiarabi-voloritorno.html

87. Pope Francis. (2020, March 25). General Audience. Retrieved from http://www.vatican.va/content/francesco/en/audiences/2020/documents/papa-francesco_20200325_udienza-generale.html

88. Pope Francis. (2020, September 10). Pope Francis: 'Never again to the culture of abuse'. *Catholic News Agency*. Retrieved from https://www.catholicnewsagency.com/news/never-

again-to-the-culture-of-abuse-says-pope-francis-in-book-
introduction-18108

89. Pope Saint John Paul II. (1992, March 25). *Vatican.*
Retrieved from http://www.vatican.va/content/john-
paul-ii/en/apost_exhortations/documents/hf_jp-
ii_exh_25031992_pastores-dabo-vobis.html

90. Pope Saint Paul VI. (1970, February 5). *The Catholic
News Archive.* Retrieved from
https://thecatholicnewsarchive.org/?a=d&d=ca1970020
5-01.2.5

91. Pope Saint Paul VI. (1967.). *Vatican.* Retrieved from
http://www.vatican.va/content/paul-
vi/en/encyclicals/documents/hf_p-
vi_enc_24061967_sacerdotalis.html

92. President Michael D. Higgins. President of the Republic
of Ireland. (2015). *Coping International.* Retrieved from
http://www.copinginternational.com/

93. Report of the Commission on Assisted Human
Reproduction. (2005). Retrieved from

https://www.lenus.ie/bitstream/handle/10147/46684/17
40.pdf;jsessionid=BD5DDFFB0C3B03601F860E9BB969
4911?sequence=1

94. Rev. Robert Kaslyn SJ. (2018, July.). *Coping International*. Retrieved from
http://www.copinginternational.com/priest/

95. Rezendes., M. (2017, August 16). A Priest's Son Takes His Case Directly to the Pope. *The Boston Globe*. Retrieved from
https://www.bostonglobe.com/metro/2017/08/17/father
-father-priest-son-takes-his-case-directly-
pope/g8ObYaoNATZy3itVSzdflM/story.html

96. Rice., D. (1992.). *Shattered Vows*. Michael Joseph/ Penguin.

97. Rice., D. (2020). Via Email.

98. Rome Reports. (2017, March). *Rome Reports*. Retrieved from https://www.youtube.com/watch?v=-gHtD-YmEIU

99. Rome Reports. (2020, August 7). *Rome Reports.* Retrieved from https://www.romereports.com/en/2020/08/07/vatican-publishes-book-on-persevering-in-and-abandoning-religious-life/

100.   Sants., H. (1964). *Wiley.* Retrieved from https://onlinelibrary.wiley.com/doi/abs/10.1111/j.2044-8341.1964.tb01981.x

101.   Sepe., C. (2020, October 19). Letter.

102.   Sepe., C. C. (n.d.). Vatican. Retrieved from http://www.vatican.va/roman_curia/congregations/ccle rgy/documents/rc_con_cclergy_doc_01011993_revel_e n.html

103.   Sister Marie McDonald. (2020., July 14). Via Email.

104.   Sr. Carmen Sammut. (2019, February 25). *Rome Reports.* Retrieved from https://www.romereports.com/en/2019/02/25/religious

-sisters-present-womens-importance-at-summit-against-abuse/

105. Standing., G. (2018, May 2). Who are 'The Precariat' and why do they threaten our society? Retrieved from https://www.euronews.com/2018/05/01/who-are-the-precariat-and-why-they-threaten-our-society-view

106. Stanford Encyclopedia of Philosophy. (n.d.). Doctrine of Double Effect. Retrieved from https://plato.stanford.edu/entries/double-effect/

107. Synod.va. (2019). *Synod.va*. Retrieved from http://www.synod.va/content/sinodoamazonico/en/news/3rd-general-congregation--overview-presented-by-vatican-news.html

108. The Right Reverend Tim Thornton Bishop at Lambeth. (2020., September. 3.). Letter from Bishop Tim Thornton.

109.   Twomey., V. (2020). *Coping International*.
Retrieved from
http://www.copinginternational.com/vaticanguidelines/

110.   UISG. (2019, September). *Union of Superiors
General*. Retrieved from
http://www.copinginternational.com/wp-
content/uploads/2019/09/UISG-September-2019..pdf

111.   UISG. (2020). Mission. Retrieved from
http://www.internationalunionsuperiorsgeneral.org/mis
sion/

112.   Vatican Secretariat of State. (2014, December.).
Letter to Vincent Doyle, Founder of Coping International.
Retrieved from
http://www.copinginternational.com/home-version-
6/his_holiness_pope_francis_2014-confirmation-
letter/#prettyPhoto[postimages]/0